Praise for *Another Chance, Maybe the Last*

"I highly recommend that all readers emerge themselves into Keleti Sanon's quest for the acknowledgement of the common heritage between African and African American people. His book, *Another Chance, Maybe the Last*, is a heartfelt invitation from an African brother who encourages us to free our minds from the misconceptions that separate us. Sanon's refreshing perspective reveals that the time is right for us to explore and embrace our connection ... ultimately becoming better people. This book is a road map toward unity." - LaTonya Branham, college administrator, adjunct professor, and author of *CultureSeek: Connecting to African and African American History* and *Spirit Seek: Words from Scriptures That Transform Your Life*

"With a kind and omniscient eye, Keleti Sanon accurately explains the feud within both the African and American cultures; the obvious misunderstanding to which he provides a solution may bridge the gap of intolerance we know so well and allow a peace which could only empower us." - Linnea Munch, writing/linguistic student at the University of Arkansas

ANOTHER CHANCE MAYBE THE LAST

RELATIONS BETWEEN AFRICAN AMERICANS AND AFRICANS

KELETI SANON

Mandingo Publishing

Another Chance Maybe the Last

© 2009 Keleti Sanon

First Paperback Edition

All rights reserved.

No part of this publication maybe reproduced, stored in a retrieval system, or transmitted in any form or by any means, electronic, mechanical, photocopying, recording or otherwise, without the prior permission of the author.

Printed in the United States.

Please visit our website at
http://www.windowofafrica.com or
http://www.keletisanon.com.

ISBN: 978-0-615-30507-3

Cover art © Keleti Sanon & Aneesah Rasheed

Published by:

Mandingo Publishing

www.mandingopublishing.com
info@mandingopublishing.com

Dedication

Family, friends, and acquaintances come into our lives for a reason. Some relationships last for a lifetime, and some last only for a season, leaving their mark upon your life and then they move on, but the person whose life is touched never forgets the impact upon his or her life.

This book is dedicated to all the people who have touched my life and made an impact in guiding me toward who I am today. I thank you for giving me a reason to write and to say what is coming from my heart. I thank you for touching my African spirit.

William Mory Sano, my son in Virginia
Xavier Sano (My first grandson)in Virginia
Moussa Traore Sanogo, my son in Chicago
Moussa Toure and Kaba Sano, my brothers in New York City
Cheick Diarra (May his body rest in peace)
Namassa Sanogo, Assita Sano, my sisters in Chicago and Philadelphia
Toure Moutaga, my brother-in-law in Philadelphia
Mariama Camara (Poupette), my niece in Little rock, Arkansas
Bourahima Fofana in Philadelphia
Djeneba Kane and the twins in Philadelphia
Kimberly Lockhart in Little Rock, Arkansas
Mamadou and Awa Diop (Dicko) in Little rock, Arkansas
Louise Yahon in Little rock, Arkansas
Michel and Shelby koffi in Little rock, Arkansas
Alexander Collins, in Jacksonville Arkansas
Frank Mills in the Bronx, New York
Sidiki Kaba in Minneapolis

To all my New York friends and coworkers who offered support in my beginning years; to the Africans and African Americans who are making an attempt to connect; and to those who write, dance, draw, sing, and dream so our next generation knows where they come from, I say thank you for realizing the importance.

There is an old Mandingo proverb that says: *"It doesn't matter how long a piece of wood has been in the river, it will never turn into a fish."* This simply means that it doesn't matter how long the African American has been here in the United States, they are still of Africa, we are all one. We cannot change our history or our heritage.

Foreword
By Marilynn Griffith

As the child of an African father and an African-American mother, I've always wanted to know more about Africa. Doing so in America, however, hasn't always been easy.

I remember children in my elementary school shouting, "She's half-African! Don't mess with her!" I didn't know why my classmates thought that "African" meant something bad. Before coming to school, I'd thought that it meant something good. I quickly learned that my fellow students expected me to swing across the room like Tarzan without notice. Frustrated, sometimes I did just that.

As I got older, there were some positive comments—"How do you say your name? That's pretty"—but for the most part, my African background was a box of fading airmail letters, the faint memory of my father's scent, and some Nigerian art in my cousin's living room. (They tell me that my father sold African art—after he got off his day job as an engineer, of course.)

Over the years, I've met a lot of people like me—African-American—but still trying to understand the hyphen. We wander in and out of African associations, chided because we don't know the language or we've never been "home." We clamor for relationships with all things African, usually including food and clothes. And then one day, we accept what we have and ask God to fill in the gaps.

In many ways, this book fills some of those gaps. Though Mr. Sanon is from Ivory Coast, the explanations about his culture have given me a new understanding about Africa as a whole. I hope this book helps all Americans understand Africa—and America—better.

Note From The Author

I became an American citizen in 1996 after coming to this country with no way to communicate, nowhere to go, and no one to help me. I struggled through the streets of New York City, carving out a life as a cab driver, car wash attendant, and security guard. My travels around the US have given me an opportunity to witness the power of the American and African connection. While my black cousins in America have offered me help in learning about this country, this book is my gift in return: a chance to bring all Africa's children together, united in color and culture.

I no longer want to meet African Americans and feel that the Atlantic Ocean divides us. Though the native African has a strange accent and different customs from the African American, we are both part of a worldwide nation of black and brown people who sprung from Africa.

It is this understanding of family and community that we Africans have to offer America. As one who came to the US with nothing and went on to graduate college twice and become an aircraft mechanic and American citizen, I extend my hand to both Africans and Americans on the pages of this book. I pray that we can come together while we still have a chance.

One Love,
Keleti Sanon

Table of Contents

CHAPTER ONE
African-American: Understanding the Divide 1

CHAPTER TWO
Africa's Lost Children: Slavery's Legacy 9

CHAPTER THREE
The Mother Land and Uncle Sam:
Discovering African Identity in America 17

CHAPTER FOUR
It Takes a Village: Traditions of Respect and Rearing 51

CHAPTER FIVE
Food and Family: The Ivorian Home 63

CHAPTER SIX
A Family Affair: African Celebrations and Culture 67

CHAPTER SEVEN
Coming to America 89

CHAPTER EIGHT
African in America: One Man's Journey 107

CHAPTER NINE
Meeting on the Middle of the Bridge 119

"We must go back and reclaim our past so that we can move forward; So we understand why and how we came to be who we are today." —Unknown

CHAPTER ONE

AFRICAN-AMERICAN: UNDERSTANDING THE DIVIDE

"How do you feel about American blacks being called African-Americans? They're not really Africans. They don't know anything about Africa."

This comment hurt me deeply and prompted questions of my own. "These people are my family, my cousins. I am honored that they would call themselves African-Americans. Why does this bother you so much?"

I never got an answer, but the question lingered in my mind, rekindling my passion to bring those of African birth and African blood together in America. It also made me reconsider what "African-American" really means and what it could mean, if we dare to redefine it.

LABELING A LEGACY

Blacks in America have been called many things since being forced onto slave ships in Africa. Some of those names were painful and humiliating. Others, like Afro-American or the more well-known term Black, sought to give black people in America the same identification with their land of origin that other hyphenated Americans had. The difference? Those other hyphenated cultures (Asian-American, Italian-American, etc.) had immigrated to US with their language, culture and customs intact. American Blacks had been purchased or captured and brought to a place where the dominant culture spent the next 400 years beating their language and land out of their memory.

Connecting with one's country of origin isn't easy when your ancestors are listed "male slave" or "female slave." And yet all people long to know where they come from. American blacks even gave themselves a name that reflects their ancestry: African-American.

It's a small but loaded word, connecting a country to a continent, reuniting through language Africa's great-great-great-great-grandchildren with their Motherland. And yet, a hyphen still separates them, symbolizing today's divide between American-born blacks and African-born immigrants. The Middle Passage was the first journey Africans had to survive. Bridging the hyphen that divides us is just as crucial.

AFRICANS IN AMERICA

According to US Census statistics, there are 1.4 million African immigrants in the US[1]. This means the number of voluntarily African immigrants may even exceed the number of Africans brought to the US as captives.[2] In the eyes of many Africans, America is a land full of successful cousins who will be like their family. What the African immigrant finds upon arrival to America, however, is often quite the opposite.

---

[1] "Yearbook of Immigration Statistics." 2007. *Department of Homeland Security.* <http://www.dhs.gov/ximgtn/statistics/publications/LPR07.shtm>.

[2] Roberts, Sam. "More Africans Enter U.S. Than in Days of Slavery." *The New York Times.* 21 Feb. 2005
<http://www.nytimes.com/2005/02/21/nyregion/21africa.html?_r=1&scp=1&sq=more%20africans%20voluntarily%20than%20slavery&st=cse>.

Though called the United States, America is still segregated in many ways, such as race, class, and culture. Each of these divisions can be a shock to outsiders who only know America through movies and media. Unlike the hostile streets of Paris or London, where an African is immediately recognized as an immigrant, the African anticipates being thought of as one of the obviously successful entertainers or athletes he's seen portrayed on international television.

Instead, he may find himself mistaken for an American black and treated with less respect than he is accustomed to. (Some Africans, like myself, like being considered as an American at first glance.) Africans quickly learn that non-blacks seem to respect Africans more than African-Americans.

As in the days of slavery, outsiders have a big impact on the relations between native Africans and American blacks. Centuries of slavery taught blacks in America to disdain anything related to Africa. To succeed, they were taught to be as "white" as possible, in appearance, speech and otherwise. The native African comes to America bent on achieving success. While he feels love for his African-American cousins, he senses that the feeling might not be mutual. He also doesn't want to do anything that will hurt his chances for success. Still, most Africans will settle in African-American communities upon arriving to the US.

Sylviane A. Diouf, a historian and researcher at the New York Public Library's Schomburg Center, explains the American view of African immigrants versus American-born blacks. "They [African immigrants] are better educated, they're here to work, to prosper, they're more compliant and don't pose a threat."[3]

This feeling may also be tied to the fact that Africans have not been as politically mobilized or concerned with slavery reparations as African Americans. Most Americans know that many African immigrants are more concerned with the politics and problems of their home countries than their continued battles with African Americans over affirmative action and other issues.

New York state, where I myself first arrived, draws the most African immigrants, but large numbers of Africans can be found in most American cities. For instance, D.C., Atlanta, Chicago, Los Angeles, Boston, and Houston have some of the largest African immigrant populations after New York City. However, Africans can also be found in great numbers in more rural states, such as Minnesota, Maine, and Oregon.

Though many arrive to see the upraised arm of the Statue of Liberty, Africans quickly learn that despite America's great possibility for progress, the minds of many of its citizens—both black and white—are not yet free. Though the immigrant will press on so that he can succeed for himself, his family and his country, he often does so while passing by his American-born black cousins, who sometimes seem still shackled in their minds and the minds of others.

As much as race is an impact, the African learns quickly that socioeconomic class is also a big factor in how a person is treated in America. If one wants to overcome the lingering stigma of being considered "black" in the US (usually meaning

---

[3] Roberts. *New York Times*.

American-born), he must only amass the right education and a significant amount of "green." Most Africans come to America for a better life, so education and prosperity are already their desire. (US African immigrants send an average of one billion dollars a year to their families and friends[4].) As they achieve, however, the gap between them and their American-born Black cousins widens, both in performance and perception.

Culture is also a huge change for Africans arriving in America. Though most Africans have seen American television, and observation of a diminutive conceptualization of African culture and resilience, the reality of how detached people are from their families can be shocking. It can be very confusing to see American-born blacks behaving the same way. Some Africans only associate with other Africans or even with people from their own country for this reason. Determined to "stay African," they separate into communities that become havens of African culture. It is this culture that can be a gift to the community of American blacks who may never know their personal African ancestry due to slavery.

Though Africans continue to rise above race, class, and cultural differences in America, they cannot avoid sharing identity with their American-born cousins. *Both* are African-American. In fact, many of the programs and policies that allow African immigrants to succeed and ascend in society are a result of efforts of American blacks. Though slavery was and continues to be a horrible legacy in American history, the efforts to redress slavery's wrongs have allowed native Africans the chance to reclaim the wealth stolen from their countries

---

[4] Roberts. *New York Times*.

through slavery and colonialism. In exchange, we bring the gift of our African culture and understanding; a gift that often goes unclaimed.

Of the 60,000 African immigrants who come to America each year, while less than the flood of immigrants from Asia and Latin America, continue to redefine the African-American identity. Along with those arriving from the Caribbean, African immigrants now make up more than 25 percent of the black population in America. In New York City, 1 in 3 blacks are foreign-born. And that's only counting the legal immigrants who usually arrive on family reunification or diversity visas. These Africans often speak English and already have a college degree. The number of illegal African immigrants is thought to be as many as four times the reported numbers.[5]

Though these statistics have exciting implications for what it means to be "black" in America, mainstream thought still considers African immigrants and American-born blacks as separate and distinct groups. This trend accentuates the hyphen in African-American, the term that continues to anger many people.

Though many immigrant groups surpass African Americans in achievement and prosperity, it can be painful for Africans to leave their cousins behind. Differences of culture and thinking, however, leave the gap between them widening.

"Historically, every immigrant group has jumped over American-born blacks," said Eric Foner, the Columbia University historian. "The final irony would be if African immigrants did, too."[6]

---

[5] Roberts. *New York Times.*
[6] Roberts. *New York Times.*

Not only would it be ironic for African immigrants to surpass American-born blacks, it would be tragic. Though history forced Africans apart, God has brought us back together. We, both African-born and American-bred blacks, must now share what is lacking with the other in regards to culture and conduct so that all of Africa's sons and daughters may rise.

While some Africans and those most commonly referred to as African Americans and/or American-born blacks may not care whether they are considered as separate groups, the reality is that our gold, amber, honey, chocolate, cinnamon, and yes, black skin will always reveal that we are one. A few generations from now, there will likely be no African and African-American. Race will have been replaced with culture. The question is will there be any African culture left in America? I hope so.

As we celebrate the achievement of electing an African-American president, all black people in America must consider that this may also signal the end of many of the programs and policies designed to undo the wrongs of slavery. In the end, we may all be left to deal with the America that faces an African arriving, something very opposite from what we expect. With the world changing both Africa and America, we have been brought together in America for such a time as this—another chance, perhaps the last.

CHAPTER TWO

AFRICA'S LOST CHILDREN: SLAVERY'S LEGACY

In most early civilizations, slavery was a reality. Africa was no different. In the beginning, slaves were used as a resource or technology for rulers to move ahead in agriculture. Prisoners of war were often taken by an opposing tribe during battles. Often the slave would adopt his captor's family as his own.

In 1482, however, slavery in Africa changed forever. Portugal built the first of many European forts on African soil, Fort Elmina.[7] From this base in the Gold Coast (Ghana), the Portuguese sailed down the coast, trading with African rulers for slaves. The Europeans offered guns and gunpowder to keep intertribal warfare—and the slaves prisoners it brought—going strong. Eventually, shipping companies even offered mercenary soldiers along with the guns. Africa had never seen such violence and bloodshed. And it was just the beginning.

What had begun as a transaction between Europeans and African rulers quickly grew beyond the rulers' control. The chiefs began to realize that slavery was a war Africa would never win—a battle for the possession of its people. In 1526,

---

[7] Haskins, James, Kathleen Benson, and Floyd Cooper. *Bound for America: the Forced Migration of Africans to the New World.* 1st ed. New York: Harper Collins, 1999.

one of the same slave rulers who had taken prisoners to be sold into slavery wrote to the King of Portugal begging him to stop taking African people from his shores. "Our country is being utterly depopulated," he wrote.[8] Again, this was just the beginning.

With Spain claiming the New World and Portugal expanding its empire, workers were needed in the Caribbean, Mexico, Central and South America, and eventually the American colonies. Sugarcane was the new crop of choice, a main ingredient for the rum loved by Europeans and the sweet luxury that brought a high price. The problem was finding cheap workers to cultivate it. European diseases and slave trading quickly killed off most of the Indians in the Caribbean and Mexico, but the Portuguese knew of other people who didn't die from European diseases and could be easily had—Africans.

Spain, the Netherlands, France, Belgium, Sweden, Prussia[9] and other European countries quickly recognized the value of the African slave—both as labor and human exports. England would follow next, along with its upstart colonists the Americans, hungry to make their name in the New World. No one knows the true number of people who died during the slave trade, but the bones of the sharks that followed the slave ships tell a story of their own.[10]

Though slaves were traded throughout Caribbean ports for many years before the American colonies joined in, the

---

[8] Haskins, Benson, and Cooper 12-14.
[9] Ramerini, Marco. "European Forts in Ghana (Gold Coast)." *Dutch Portugues Colonial History*. 3 Jul 2009 <http://www.colonialvoyage.com/ghana.html>.
[10] Rediker, Marcus. *The Slave Ship: A Human History*. 1st. New York: Viking Adult, 2007.

demand for "darkies" compelled many businessmen to start shipping companies to transport the world's best-selling commodity—Africans. No one needed free labor more than the English colonies in America. The captains of slave ships turned their boats into floating factories, turning Africans into slaves before reaching the New World.[11]

The players in the evil that became the Transatlantic Slave Trade were many; some of them were being exploited as well without realizing it: the poor white slave sailors who would translate into the overseers of the same class once the ship reached shore; the millions of naked slaves stripped of home and dignity in the ship's bowels; the African kings and rulers who traded their prisoners and enemies for the possibility of power; and finally the white politicians, slave owners and merchants back in America who refused to soil their ruffles with the blood of the millions[12] lost to Transatlantic slavery, but relished in profiting from it.[13]

Just as in today's trafficking of women and children from underdeveloped countries, sadly, there has always been a price upon the lives of those who cannot afford to defend themselves. The American Indian chiefs were wooed with the same gunpowder and trinkets used on African leaders. While these items would later cost the Native Americans everything, at first these things were very appealing to those who have never seen them.

What happened to our cousins in America was—and is—horrible. We learn about it in school and mourn the loss of so

---

[11] Rediker, Marcus 1-2.
[12] Franklin, John Hope. *From Slavery to Freedom: A History of African Americans.* 8th. New York: Knopf, 2000.
[13] Rediker.

many of our African family. However, the horrors of slavery were just the beginning of what European powers had in store for Africa.

The same African leaders who had given over captives to slavers would soon see their lands taken over by England, France, Spain, and other European powers. Africa's inheritance—her gold, diamonds, oil, and people—were stolen and given to other countries while Africa watched its freedom and resources fade.

Both the American slave and those left behind in Africa watched as others became rich off their backs and land and left them with nothing. Some sorrowed so much at the loss of family and future that they never made it to the New World. They jumped or were thrown overboard. The Africans who made the journey determined to stay alive and to keep Africa alive in their hearts. Our ancestors would want for all Africa's children, no matter where they were born, to do the same.

Slavery robbed African Americans of the language, land, and legacy of Africa. I cannot replace those things, but I can share my own culture and country with you and ask that African Americans not be angry with us for the actions of some greedy men long ago. Instead be angry with the corrupt thinking that still threatens us today. There was no winner in what happened to Africa. Whether one was carried away or left behind, all have lost something precious. We must come together now and seek to regain it.

LIBERIA: AN AFRICAN-AMERICAN COLONY

While President Abraham Lincoln is applauded for emancipating the American slaves in 1862, it was not necessarily because he wanted to end slavery.

"If I could save the Union without freeing any slave I would do it, and if I could save it by freeing all the slaves I would do it..." [14] Lincoln said on one occasion.

What really concerned Lincoln—and the vast majority of white Americans—was the possibility of a freed slave uprising. Like most people of the time, Lincoln himself could not accept the concept of equal treatment for blacks and whites:

"...Make them [Negroes] politically and socially, our equals? My own feelings will not admit of this; and if mine would, we well know that those of the great mass of white people will not,"[15] Lincoln said in a speech in 1854.

Lincoln was right. Though most slave owners had children from slave women, the thought of equality between the two races was unthinkable to them. Their solution would be to send the slaves back to Africa.

In 1817, the American Colonization Society (ACS) was formed with the support of Kentucky politician Henry Clay; Francis Scott Key, author of The Star Spangled Banner; Bushrod Washington, nephew of President George Washington and Supreme Court Justice; and William Thornton,

---

[14] Randall, Vernellia. "Lincoln on Slavery." *Race, Racism and the Law.* University of Dayton Law School. 3 Jul 2009
<http://academic.udayton.edu/race/02rights/slave07.htm#Free%20them>.
[15] "Lincoln on Slavery."

architect of the U.S. Capitol.[16] All were slave owners with moderate politics. Quakers also supported the effort, believing emancipation of slaves impossible.

Land in Africa was purchased from local tribes for the purpose of creating a colony for slave owners to ship their slaves back to. In 1822, approximately 86 freed slaves voluntarily boarded a ship bound for Africa. Over the next 40 years, almost 20,000 former slaves would arrive in Liberia.[17]

One Liberian settler, Revered Lott Cary, left a pastorate of over 800 free blacks in Richmond, Virginia, to go to Liberia. When asked why he went, Lott replied, "I am an African, and in this country, however meritorious my conduct, and respectable my character, I cannot receive the credit due to either. I wish to go to a country where I shall be estimated by my merits, not by my complexion; and I feel bound to labor for my suffering race."[18]

Though Cary had more than most blacks at the time, including his freedom, he identified himself clearly as African. This same type of connection to Africa is possible for the African American today. Reach out and connect with a heritage deeply rooted within. Imagine what can happen if we use the freedom we have today to help and support each other and Africa.

---

[16] Ricks, Mary Kay. "Who Founded Liberia?" *Slate Magazine*. 03 July 2003 <http://www.slate.com/id/2085169/pagenum/all/>.

[17] Duva, Anjali Mitter. "The Lone Star: The Story of Liberia." *Global Connections: Liberia*. 2002. PBS. 3 Jul. 2009 <http://www.pbs.org/wgbh/globalconnections/liberia/essays/history/index.html>.

[18] "The Lone Star: The Story of Liberia."

Lack of support, conflict with local tribes, disease and dissent led to the collapse of the American Colonization Society. No one wanted to declare American sovereignty on African soil, so they declared Liberia "free" and abandoned it, making Liberia the oldest nation in Africa to gain independence.

In Liberia today, there are remnants of those who made the voyage of their ancestors—in the opposite direction. The Liberian capital is called Monrovia, after American President James Monroe. Five percent of today's Liberian population is descended from the American slaves who settled Liberia, many of whom are among the nation's high-ranking people.[19] The Liberian flag looks much like the American flag, except that there is one star instead of fifty small ones. The hope that was Liberia represents the unity and love that Africans can have again: One star, one love, and one Africa.

---

[19] Robert, Patrick. "Liberia and America: A Photo Journal." *Time Magazine*. 3 Jul. 2009 <http://www.time.com/time/photoessays/patrickrobert/>.

CHAPTER THREE

THE MOTHER LAND AND UNCLE SAM: DISCOVERING AFRICAN IDENTITY IN AMERICA

People who have never even visited Africa have portrayed it as "the dark continent," ignoring the beautiful side of Africa, such as its diversity, learning, and resourcefulness.

To see Africa's light, we must look past the veil imposed by slavery and colonialism. Here are some quick facts about Africa that are often misunderstood:

- **Africa is a continent, not a country.**

There are 53 countries in Africa. It is the second largest continent in the world, both in area and population. (Asia is the first). Despite the perception by some in the West of one giant safari full of lions and savages, Africa is a continent rich in people (the population is over 1 billion) and resources (the oil rush continues in Africa) with many large cities such as Abidjan, the second-largest French speaking city in the world with over 5 million residents, in my native Ivory Coast.

- **All Africans do not look the same.**

Within Africa, there are hundreds of dialects, tribes and people groups. Some, like the Arabic-speaking Africans of northern Africa would be considered Middle Eastern; however, their roots are in Africa. They are no less African because they aren't dark-skinned or don't speak an "African" language. Throughout the continent there are all types of beautiful, intelligent people who speak many languages.

The first African-American, Estevanico the Black (or the Moor), was from Morocco in northern Africa.[20] He visited Florida with a Spanish expedition in 1528. Estevanico had either been sold to or captured by Spanish soldiers in 1513 and became the slave of a Spanish nobleman who joined an expedition to the New World.[21]

- **There is more to Africa than hunger.**

While it's true that hunger is an issue in Africa, it's not because Africa is lacking in natural resources. Many African countries were European colonies as recent as the 1960s. Lack of infrastructure and political unrest has caused problems for Africans, but the continent remains the gem that drew the world's attention.

Today's draw to Africa isn't men and women for slave ships though. It's oil. At one point, Nigeria imported more oil to the US than from Saudi Arabia.[22] With many poor countries allowing agreements for developed companies to search for oil, we can expect the great oil race to speed up in Africa. Unfor-

---

[20] Terrell, John Upton. *Estevanico the Black*. Los Angeles: Westernlore Press, 1968.
[21] Heard, J. Norman. *The Black Frontiersman: Adventures of Negroes of American Native Americans (1528-1918)*. New York: The John Day Company, 1969. 1-2.
[22] Ghazvinian, John. *Untapped: The Scramble for African Oil*. New York: Harcourt, 2007.

tunately, the hunger and hardship of many will continue to be a reality.

- **Everyone in Africa does not speak Swahili.**

Swahili is widely spoken in Kenya, Tanzania, Uganda, and other countries, but there is no one language spoken across the continent. Of the almost 900 million Africans (2005), about 10% speak Swahili. Swahili is a lingua francae, or third language, often used by two people who do not share a common language. Trade languages sometimes develop into wider use this way. However, in countries like my native Ivory Coast or neighboring Nigeria, French, English and any number of regional languages are spoken.

Swahili has been prominently used in American cultural celebrations like Kwanzaa, raising the awareness of Swahili among African-Americans. We are proud and thankful for our cousin's desire to know African languages although all of us do not speak Swahili. So…Jambo!

AFRICAN GEOGRAPHY
NORTHERN AFRICA

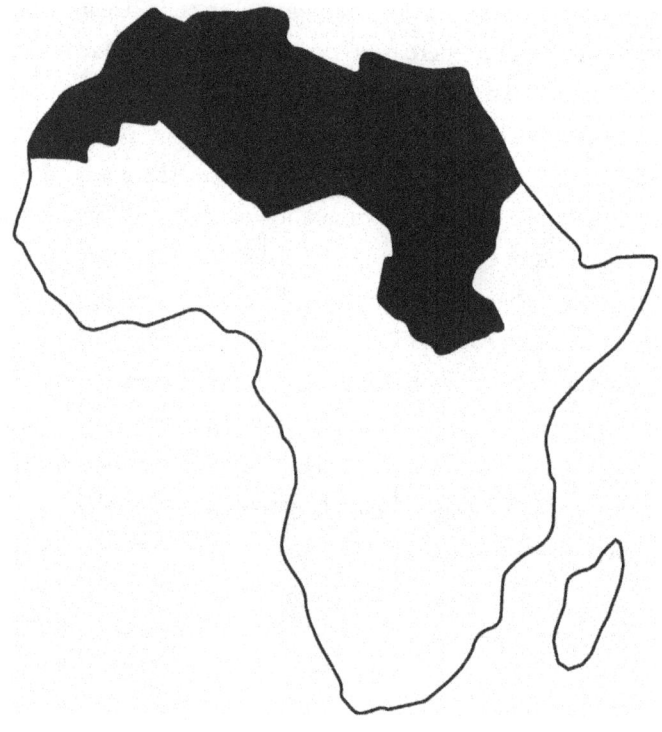

Algeria, Egypt, Libya, Morocco, Sudan, Tunisia and Western Sahara make up Northern Africa. These countries are part of what we in the US call the Muslim world and are often shown on maps of the Middle East because of this. Some African-American children have only seen Egypt on a map of the Middle East and were taught it was not a part of Africa. While the cultural differences in parts of Africa are great, we are all Africans. However, around the world the term African is often equated with dark skin, curly or kinky hair and the infamous Swahili.

Arabs invaded this region in the sixth century and like the rest of Africa, this area was under some form of European colonial rule for many years. Strictly by geography this area is African but politics, religion and culture define it as Arabic. No matter where you cut the map or what you call the people of this region, their roots are African.

That said, you would not likely see a lot of people from Northern Africa in other regions of Africa. Though they are part of Africa, these Arabic countries seem content to stay within their own region. I have never personally visited this area, but I have met many citizens from Northern African countries during my time as a security guard in New York City. I was fairly close friends with a co-worker from Morocco who people often thought to be of Spanish descent because of his light skin color. This skin color seems to be common for people from the region of Northern Africa.

EASTERN AFRICA

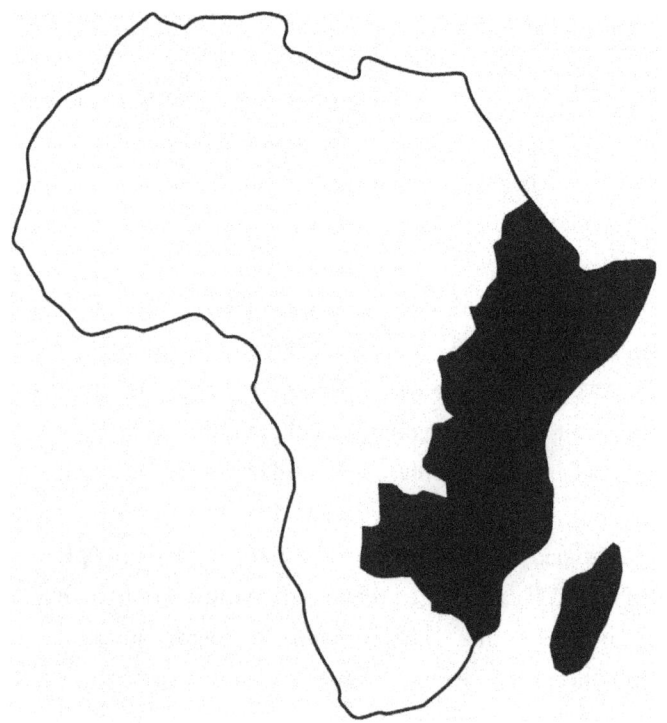

According to the United Nations geographical regions, East Africa is comprised of: Burundi, Comoros, Djibouti, Eritrea, Ethiopia, Kenya, Madagascar, Malawi, Mauritius, Mayotte, Mozambique, Reunion, Rwanda, Seychelles, Uganda, the United Republic of Tanzania, Zambia, and Zimbabwe.[23]

This is the area where the earliest human remains were found. It's considered by many scientists to be the birthplace of humanity. This area is also known for its wildlife in the past, but populations of elephants, lions and other species have declined in recent years. Though the low lying regions are very dry, there are also several mountains and very wet regions with a lot of rainfall. This area also contains the headwaters of the Nile and Congo Rivers, both named in the Bible and known throughout history. According to the National Geographic Human Fingerprint Map, there are millions of farms in this region. As a continent, however, Africa still only uses 3 percent of the world's electricity.[24]

Though Portugal was one of the first European countries to trade in this region, countries from all over the world vied to control parts of this area during the colonial period. Unfortunately, Eastern Africa is most known to many Americans for its wars in Darfur, Sudan; Ethiopia, and Uganda or the famous movie *Hotel Rwanda* with African-American actor Don Cheadle. While there have been ugly things that have happened

---

[23] "Composition of Macro Geographical (Continental) Regions, Geographical Sub-Regions, and Selected Economic and Other Groupings." *United Nations Statistics Division Standard Country and Area Codes.* United Nations, Web. 16 Sept. 2009
<http://millenniumindicators.un.org/unsd/methods/m49/m49regin.htm>.
[24] "Atlas Explorer, African Human Footprint Map." *National Geographic.* 16 Sept. 2009 <http://maps.nationalgeographic.com/maps/atlas/africa-human-footprint.html>.

in this area, there are many beautiful, loving people in these countries, especially children.

This is another region that I have not visited personally, but have met a lot of people from Eastern African countries. It seems that every time I meet someone from this region, we socialize and become friends. They always invite me to their ceremonies (weddings, graduations, national independence parties, etc.). There is a lot of similarity between their culture and traditions and those of my own Ivory Coast. The people from this region that I've met are very courageous people with a strong ambition to develop their countries back at home and help their people with education and health care.

CENTRAL OR MIDDLE AFRICA

Though African people often view themselves tribally, outsiders have always divided Africa regionally. The current divisions of countries considered by the United Nations as Middle Africa are Angola, Central African Republic, Chad, Democratic Republic of the Congo, Cameroon, Equatorial Guinea, Gabon and Sao Tome and Principe. These countries along with Burundi and Rwanda (formerly considered as Central Africa) comprise the Economic Community of Central African States (ECCAS).[25]

This area of the continent is very warm and has a lot of rain forests. The Congo River takes up a lot of this region. I have had the chance to visit this region several times. I have been to Gabon where my ex-wife is from, as well as Cameroon and Guinea Equatorial, which is one of the official Spanish-speaking countries in Africa. That was very interesting to learn. This region has been well known for decades for bringing new styles of dance and clothing onto streets all over Africa.

I remember watching a show on TV when I was a kid with almost everyone from the compound. The performers were from Zaire, Congo, and Cameroon. These performers planted a seed in the entertainment industry in black or sub-Saharan Africa because even now their style of music is still very popular in many bars, clubs, wedding parties, and TV dance parties.

---

[25] "Economic Community of Central African States." *Regional Economic Communities.* African Union, Web. 23 Sept. 2009 <http://www.africa-union.org/root/au/recs/eccas.htm>.

WESTERN AFRICA

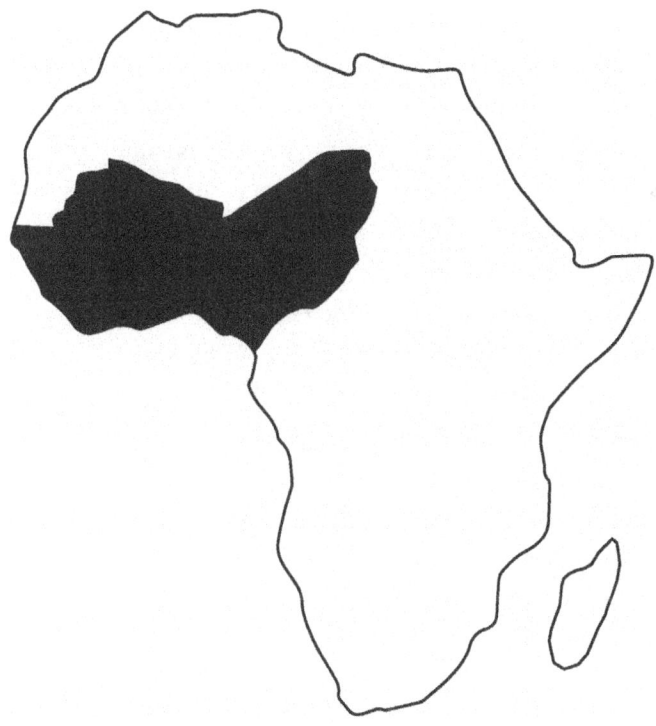

The countries classified in this region are: Benin, Burkina Faso, Cape Verde, Cote d'Ivoire (Ivory Coast), Gambia, Ghana, Guinea, Guinea-Bissau, Liberia, Mali, Mauritania, Niger, Nigeria, Saint Helena, Senegal, Sierra Leone, and Togo.

This area is my region. There are at least seven countries that have Mandingo tribes spread throughout regions with other tribes. The boundaries of countries in this region are often colonial boundaries. They do not accurately represent the tribal connections of the people. This continues to be a problem long after the independence of many nations. I am very familiar with almost all the citizens of these countries as well as their culture, religion, food, and behavior. This area is bordered above by the Sahara Desert and to the west and below by the Atlantic Ocean.

I grew up around people from this region and was welcomed to the US by people from this area. I have a few dozen friends from this region that I spend time sharing celebrations with. Being with them is like being at home back in Africa, only in America.

SOUTHERN AFRICA

The countries in this area are: Botswana, Lesotho, Namibia, South Africa, and Swaziland. There is also the Southern African Development Community [26] comprised of Angola, Botswana, Democratic Republic of the Congo, Lesotho, Madagascar, Malawi, Mauritius, Mozambique, Namibia, South Africa, Swaziland, Tanzania, Zambia, and Zimbabwe. This is another example of how political boundaries contradict cultural ones as many of these countries are categorized by the United Nations under different regions of Africa.

This area has grasslands, flatlands, and deserts and is known to be rich in platinum. There are still large numbers of the wildlife Africa is known for in this region, such as lions, rhinoceros, and leopards. Due to colonization, there are large numbers of people from European and Asian descent in this area.

I have never visited this region myself, but thanks to the US, I have met many people from this area. As a matter of fact, I'm still in contact with some of them after 18 years. The people of Southern Africa are very determined and ambitious people, and I have a lot in common with their culture and traditions.

Overall, I have visited only eight countries, including my own: Ivory Coast, Mali, Burkina Faso, Guinea, Gabon, Nigeria, Cameroon, and Guinea Equatorial. By coming to America and living here for over twenty years, I have met many Africans from over 30 different communities in countries I never visited while in Africa.

---

[26] "Towards a Common Future." *Southern African Development Community.* SADC. 23 Sept. 2009 <http://www.sadc.int/>.

In the US, however, Africans from other countries have been my co-workers, fellow students, and neighbors. These relationships allowed me to ask questions about each person's respective country and culture. It is interesting to see the similarities and differences in our culture.

I have participated in many ceremonies here in America that was rooted in the cultures of African countries I have never visited: weddings, graduation parties, birthdays, etc. In many ways, a person can visit Africa by getting to know the Africans in America. The US is truly a melting pot, and for all of us to be here together and get to know each other is a real gift. We are living a part of history right now.

ABOUT IVORY COAST

I am from Ivory Coast in West Africa. My country got its name from European Ivory traders who came to the area centuries ago. There were also other "coasts" in Africa. There was the Gold Coast (Ghana), the Grain Coast (Liberia) and unfortunately, the Slave Coast (Republic of Benin and Togo). My country gained its independence from France in 1960, but we kept the name we had become known by.

There are many rain forests, mountains, and woodlands in my country. There are over 15 million people living there. My land is about the size of the state of New Mexico. There are many new economic initiatives in Ivory Coast, but much of our wealth has come from minerals, oil, coffee, cocoa, and other agricultural products. The Ivory Coast ranks third in the world in coffee production, exceeded only by Brazil and Columbia.

In the good days of Ivory Coast with the first president Felix Houphouet Boigny, the stability and prosperity of the country was amazing. Many people were relocating to the Ivory Coast, and jobs were everywhere. New companies were coming to Ivory Coast from all over Europe, and investors were investing in construction, roads, housing, trade and other commodities. The worldwide economic downturn has affected growth everywhere, but Ivorian natives all over the world, me included, are doing what we can to reinvest in Ivory Coast and help support economic development there.

REDISCOVERING AFRICAN IDENTITY IN AMERICA

Conversations with African Americans have taught me the grim lesson of how successful slave owners were at destroying the African identity. Many American-born blacks view Africa as a place of people with little or no intelligence—the same way whites once viewed them. African Americans have struggled so hard to overcome the lies of segregation, racism, and slavery that perhaps they began to believe some of the lies about Africa along the way.

Though many Africans come to the US and study hard in challenging disciplines, the African American is still seen as separate from this root of intellect and hard work. Children who get good grades or speak proper English are often termed as "acting white" by their peers as though black people—African people—around the world have not been doing just that for a very long time.

To control a nation of people, the first step is to take away their language, then their history and sadly, their families. While many slaves were sold away from their immediate families, they were shamed, beaten, and taken away from their extended African families as well. For this reason, I encourage every African American to visit some part of Africa at least once in his or her life to see firsthand the good and the bad. Some media sources have been successful at keeping Africa and the African-American apart for centuries. We cannot let this continue.

Today's children do not sit at the knee of an elder hearing their heritage, but rather perch at the foot of a television blaring out the names of the next pop star or rap song. Young Americans, white and black alike, are bombarded with false images of people involved in sex, violence, drugs, and worse. Everyone wants to keep up with the Joneses and stay in the in-crowd. We must stop focusing on peer relationships for our children and look to family, church, and community for guidance.

Though technology is a great asset, history and culture are also powerful tools for shaping the future. Instead of worrying about the latest song or video, let's talk to our young people about leadership, world news, and politics. Take a trip, record an oral history with the elders in your family, trace your genealogy. Let's expand our children's minds across the world, all the way to Africa.

KENTE CLOTH AND BEYOND

Knowing ourselves is important. It gives us a sense of identity, dignity, and community. Many African Americans know this well and spend lots of money and time trying to educate themselves and their families about Africa. However, the sources are not African! For far too long, others have told us who we are. It is time to find out about ourselves for ourselves.

Slavery taught African Americans to deny Africa. This wound is so deep that some American blacks do not feel connected with the land they sprung from. Still others think that wearing cornrows and kente cloth is all that's needed to understand Africa. That, too, is a mistake. Africa's roots are deeper than any hairstyle or outfit. Though some are sincere, there are also fashion fads that pretend to return to African roots only to switch to another trend soon after.

While clothing and hairstyles can be powerful symbols of African solidarity, embracing Africa goes deeper than the outer appearance into the mind. For some, it will take a time of allowing themselves to feel the pain of slavery and the joy of the forgiveness before embracing the beauty of Africa. When we get down to the real questions of purpose and who we are trying to please and impress and what we can pass on to those coming behind us, the African mindset will bloom.

Though there are many cultures throughout Africa, we all share a concept of family, success, and future. We know what is expected of us as African men and women, and we don't hesitate to deliver, especially in our responsibility to our families. For the most part, we know who we are and live accordingly.

This hidden determination is not what is valued in the West. Here, a person can appear to have African pride while it is nothing more than pretense. The African may lack the material things America is looking for, but his head is held high, even in the darkest moments of his life. He knows the difference between his true self and the images created by someone's imagination. He rejects those ideals and replaces them with the reality of who he is and what he must do. Regardless of the situation, the true African is known by more than an accent, food, or dress. His identity is authentic. You can see it in his eyes, hear it in his tone, and see it in his walk… He is African.

DAYS OF DISCOVERY

Each year, our children attend approximately 180 days of school. What are they doing the rest of the year? Yank out their headphones and unplug the game consoles and plan at least one day a year as a day of discovery into their African heritage. Here are a few things you can do to make this happen.

- EXPLORE AN EXPO.
  Many major cities in the US have a Black Expo during the summer months. These events are usually held in a large convention center over a span of several days. There are usually celebrities, authors, businesses, music, information, and celebration of African-American culture. If there isn't a Black Expo or African Festival in your community, con-

sider organizing one as a family and coordinating it through your city or county. Sometimes all a good idea is lacking are the feet to get it moving!

Visit http://www.indianablackexpo.com and http://www.blackexpousa.com for just a few of the events across the nation.

- ORAL HISTORY.
  Think about your grandparents, great-grand parents and so on. How much do you really know about them? Interview your oldest living relative about anything they want to tell you. Though they may be generations removed from Africa, listen for her in their stories. As in your own life story, she will be there. We must train ourselves to know where to look and how to hear the voices of our ancestors.

  If possible, record the interview digitally and allow your child to ask some of the questions. This is something they can show their own children in the years to come. Need some help with this idea? Contact Story Corps (http://storycorps.org), a nonprofit oral history project, to rent recording equipment, Story Kit, or download their interview guidelines.

- DRAW THE LINE.
  Nothing can express the beauty of Africa's history and landscape like African art. There are many African-American artists who spend their lives portraying the col-

ors, shapes, and symbols of the human experience through Africa's eyes. Let your children choose a piece to start your family collection. Buy inexpensive prints as well and quiz your children throughout the year on the names and styles of the different artists. The National Black Arts Festival (http://nbaf.org) conducts year-round tours and events, including the festival each July.

Some sites your family might enjoy include:

- Aakofii, jewelry (http://www.aakofii.com)
- Abiola (http://www.abiolaartgallery.com)
- African American Artists (http://www.artcyclopedia.com/nationalities/African-American.html)
- Charles Bibbs (http://www.theworldart.com)
- Woodrow Nash, Creative Nouveau Ceramics (http://www.theragegallery.com)
- Roederick Vines, Vines Art (http://www.vinesart.com)
- Three Generations of African-American Women Sculptors (http://www.tfaoi.com/newsmu/nmus66b.htm)

- STIR THE POT
  Many of today's soul food traditions have African cuisine at their root. Take your family on a culinary field trip, choosing a soul food lunch and a dinner at a traditional African restaurant. Ask your children what was different

and the same about the two meals. See if they can figure out how some of the dishes might have originated. Buy or checkout several cookbooks from the local library. Give them a budget and let them help buy ingredients and prepare a meal for friends, family or classmates. Invite an African family in your neighborhood or church to dinner and ask them to bring their favorite dish.

- CALL THE NAME.
  Whenever your family meets an African person, ask them the spelling and meaning of their name and record in a notebook. Take a day to look through the names and their meanings and ask your children to choose a new name for a day. Encourage them to name their toys and pets African names and when visitors ask about the names, let your children explain the meanings of the names they have chosen. Instead of having a dog or doll named Billy Bob or Bonnie, try Bakari or Bimkubwa! Your child will always have a conversation starter around the house.

- CRUISE THE CARIBBEAN.
  Though you may not have the finances to travel to Africa right away, the influence of Africa is still easily seen in the Caribbean. Take a one-day cruise with your family and tour some of the first sites our ancestors saw after leaving home. To save costs on passports, visit the US Virgin Islands (St. Croix, St. John, and St. Thomas). These islands are American territories and no passport is required to visit.

Our African family is an open book ... even if some of the pages are missing. Determine to start a new chapter in sharing your heritage with your children and your community.

If you are an African immigrating to America, bring all of Africa with you when you come. Though you cannot bring everyone or everything from home physically, bring everything with you in your heart. Don't trade the diamond of your culture in for the plastic toy or friendship or success. Don't barter your ethics away for opportunity. If you do, you may find yourself unable to buy them back.

Instead, help your fellow Americans rediscover Africa. If you change who you are, some people may never know Africa as she truly is—pure and beautiful. Succeed. Celebrate. Just don't try to fall into the trap of trying to be something you're not.

SHADES OF SHAME

Another product of slavery and colonization is the concept of European-based beauty. Images of black women who look more Caucasian than African have become the only standard of beauty in America and around the world. Fashion, music, and advertising choose the most white-looking models or entertainers again and again, leaving young African-American girls hating themselves and young African-American boys judging their sisters by the standards they can never meet. We must let all women know that they don't need blond hair or blue eyes to be beautiful.

In Africa, strong, beautiful women are everywhere, draped in bright African clothing, carrying things on their regal heads crowned with kinky hair. This is the beauty that we must once again celebrate and reclaim, though, even some African women have begun to think black is not beautiful. Even my African sisters bleach their skin to be more acceptable in today's society. They also walk around with long, flowing straight hair on their heads that looks as though it belongs on a mannequin. This is a shame and makes me very sad.

The children are doing it, too. Young black children imitate celebrities like Hannah Montana and those from *High School Musical*. The sad truth is that while we invest our time and money into America's mainstream pop culture, it is Caucasians who are imitating African beauty. Today's bronzers and tanning beds produce dark skin and injections and padding produce full lips and rounded curves. Why are we trading places, leaving women from all cultures to believe they should be something other than what they are? Everyone seems to be trying to find something unique in a culture other than their own. This trend has cultivated depression and discontent in many women and failed relationships for many men.

We must rejoice in who we are. Remember James Brown's "I'm Black and I'm Proud"? That song wasn't just about skin color, but something even deeper. Back then, African pride was displayed with afros and dashikis; today's trend is dreadlocks and kente cloth. Regardless of the outward expression, let the message sink deep into your soul—black is beautiful.

As for dreadlocks, while worn by the Egyptians in northern Africa and dated back to the Nazirites of Biblical times, countries in sub-Saharan Africa, such as where I am from, don't favor this hairstyle. Ethiopians and other African countries have a tradition of dreadlocks, but many people associate this with Jamaica and the Rastafarian religion. Returning to one's natural hair is a good thing, but dreadlocks are worn by people all over the world and are not necessarily African.

Let's respect our God-given characteristics and traits instead of trying to change them. How many cultures do you know spend hundreds of dollars each month to look like someone else? And let's not even talk about the time involved. If the average Caucasian woman had to get up every day and make her straight hair kinky and get it braided into cornrows, she would never be able to make it out her door!

Other cultures are making a living off of selling us the goods of European beauty. Think about what would happen if we used that same money to visit Africa or buy books to educate ourselves. Learning to love our African identity may be hard for some, but keep pressing on until you see yourself for the queen or king that you are. Refuse to be the puppets of large corporations who benefit from selling products and services to those with a slavery mindset. Invest that time and money into your family and community.

While Africa may not be as modern a continent as North America, Africans try to remain true to who we are. However, even Africans fall into the trap of trying to look like someone we can never be—and shouldn't want to be. This system is another type of oppression, one that leaves black people unhappy with how they look and wondering how they should act. Unsatisfied, they work harder and harder to fit into the idea of beauty and success in the West, sometimes losing parts of their souls along the way.

COLOR CONFLICTS

Even in the new millennium, the lighter skinned you are in America, the better. Slaves were pitted against each other and taught that the closer to being white a person was, the better he was. (Forget the rape and humiliation that gave him this lighter color.) Sally Hemmings, a slave of President Thomas Jefferson who bore him many children who are only now being recognized as his descendants, is evidence of how big a lie that was. Despite their light color, neither President Jefferson's slave children nor their mother were given freedom upon his death.[27]

This poisonous "the lighter the better" thinking even confuses people's understanding of African skin coloring. When I try to tell some African Americans that there are tribes in Africa who are naturally light-skinned without any mixing with Europeans, they rarely believe me. My nephew in Chicago is very light-skinned. Both his parents are full-blooded Africans.

The color conflict goes back to the slave owners' need to believe that Africans were less than human. In their minds, only white blood bestowed intellect. When we fall for this faulty thinking, we are once again embracing the chains of our captors. We must free our minds concerning preferential treatment according to skin color. Mental slavery can continue the cycle of captivity long after a people are free.

---

[27] "Jefferson's Blood." *PBS*. PBS. 4 Aug. 2009
<http://www.pbs.org/wgbh/pages/frontline/shows/jefferson/>.

BRINGING AFRICA BACK INTO AMERICA

Though millions of slaves were brought to America, we now find ourselves with a generation of young people often lacking identity. We must go back and fetch it, as some say. If you are of African descent, you are African. Whether it is part of your heritage or all of it, doesn't give up your identity for anyone. Be proud of your African heritage, no matter what you see or hear on TV. We may not all have the wealth of the western world, but we have a wealth of understanding and innovativeness. Research your own family tree and start saving to come to Africa and see the land we all came from.

Slavery and colonialism is over, but the mental and psychological effects continue. We must daily shake the chains off our minds and struggle to accept each other and our African heritage. Some want to be "just American" to make others more comfortable, but don't buy into that lie either.

Immigrants come to America from all over the world and celebrate and share their culture. Americans are eager to discover the culture of people immigrating to America, including Africans. African-American culture, however, can be a sore subject with some, especially after the election of Barack Obama in 2008. Many Americans feel that this election fulfilled anything still lacking to the descendants of slaves. This is a dangerous trend. One reason that the Jewish people never stop talking about The Holocaust is so that it will never happen again. We must not be afraid to face the legacy of slavery in this country and the forgiveness and focus required to move forward. We don't have to dwell on the past, but we can come together and celebrate the future of both Africa and America.

As it says in the Holy Bible, "Seek and ye shall find" (Matthew 7:7, KJV). Our native hands are reaching out to our American cousins. Our roots are your roots. Use this book and the Africans in your community to uncover the gift of Africa that is yours for the taking. Dig deeper and see the truth.

DEALING WITH DIFFERENCES

To bridge the divide between Africans and black Americans, we must both acknowledge our stereotypes and reject them. We must admit that we have grown to like, or even love, some of the things that oppress us. We must also accept that some people have removed themselves from any connection with Africa and will never face their own true selves.

Though misinformation is hard to overcome, it can be done. We would not go to Alaska or Jamaica to learn about Korean culture. We must stop doing the same when it comes to Africa. To truly learn more about whom we are and where we come from, we—Africans and African Americans—will have to come together.

Some feel disconnected from Africa because the media images show conditions they could never live in. True enough, there are some hard things going on in Africa, but consider this: How can the African people stand so proud and meek in such adversity? Why are we always happy to return home, even once we are citizens in the US? We always keep Africa in our hearts. She is in our blood, in our mindsets. Perhaps it was this strength and determination which kept the slaves alive under circumstances which should have killed them. Perhaps it is this mindset which will return African-American culture to the dignity and respect it deserves.

CARIBBEAN CONNECTION

As I stated before, some remnants of African culture continue in the Caribbean even today. For this reason, it is often easier for African immigrants to connect with their Caribbean brothers and sisters. Some Caribbean women still wear their babies on their backs and carry things on their heads. In the West, the only thing a black woman is taught to wear on her head is a graduation cap—which is a great thing, but not the only thing. Instead of a baby on her back, the African-American woman is taught to push her baby in a metal stroller while carrying the weight of the world on her back.

While we know that most African-American women won't start carrying things on their heads or wearing their babies on their backs necessarily, research it though to learn the traditions. These are some things we have in common with our Caribbean cousins. Even some of their languages such as Creole and others still contain some of the language of West Africa. In the Gullah area of South Carolina, some African folktales are still told and many African dishes are prepared under new names. While we dream that every one of Africa's lost sons and daughters will one day visit home, visiting the Caribbean can also give insight into the African culture before slavery. Caribbean people experience some part of Africa on a daily basis.

NATIVE NOTIONS

While the American Indian was stripped of his land and everything he'd ever had, Native Americans still preserve their culture, even down to keeping track of the members and descendants of each tribe. They know their history and celebrate and remain proud of it, despite the horrible things that were done to them on the Trail of Tears. They pass along their stories to their children.

African Americans must begin to do this also, especially considering the recent decisions of some Native tribes to expel the blacks from their tribal rolls.[28] It is time now to bring the Africans' horrible trip to America full circle. Though this is now our home, Africa must always be in our hearts.

A LEGACY OF LOVE

On a personal note, let me share something with you, Africa's children, young and old. You are a blessed people. Do not let anyone tell you different. The world refuses to see that we have a gift from God because they already think less of us, but we are gifted in many ways. I pray that you will hear me and wake up to the truth of who you are!

I have been back to Africa many times since becoming a citizen and each time, I see Africa slowly trickling away. As a Mandingo man, I see the disruption of tradition, culture, village

---

[28] Lee, Jeninne. "The Cherokee Nation's New Battle." *Time Magazine*. 4 Aug. 2009 <http://www.time.com/time/nation/article/0,8599,1635873,00.html>.

life, and the values of my country, Ivory Coast, eroding, becoming westernized and Americanized.

It is not only African Americans who are losing touch with home. African children born to African parents in America, parents who came to this rich country with Africa imprinted on their very spirit, are being raised no different than their American neighbors. As so much African culture was once lost to slavery, Africa is turning to dust again as our hands reach for the TV remote while dreaming of the next best thing the world says we should have.

Though Africans come to this country to better ourselves and African-Americans want to continue their legacy of overcoming and achieving, we cannot forget who we are and where we come from in the process of bettering ourselves. Trying too hard to fit in and become like everyone else can keep us from preserving our heritage.

If you are an African living in America, rejoice when your children speak English but speak to them in your native language as well, helping them to never forget Africa. Language should always be preserved. My sister speaks in Mandingo to her son. He answers her in English. Both share the best of both worlds, African and American.

Clothing is important, too. Let's trade in the sagging pants and overpriced jeans for clothing that embraces our heritage. Go to the store this weekend and look and listen. Does the Mexican stop speaking Spanish when he arrives? Does the Indian woman wear only western style clothing? Do the Chinese stop communicating in their language or preserving their culture? No. We Africans must not be any different.

Though we have been separated by hyphens and oceans, we must come back together once more.

The world is once again changing. Africa as we have known it will one day cease to exist, extinct like some wild beast, preserved only through the eyes of others. This will happen not only because of the chaos and turmoil plaguing the continent but because the citizens of Africa have forgotten their culture, traditions, and language. It will happen because a generation of children will enter adult life not knowing who they really are, missing the value and culture of Africa that defines us as a people.

We must not allow our legacy to be reduced to statues in a museum. All African Americans must "pass it on" through stories, oral history, books, travel, and connection with the world. Though we want to bury the hurts of slavery, we must not kill Africa in the process. Africa is more than just skin color, and its culture is more than just skin deep. We will need the support of all people with a heart for Africa to support the cultural expressions which help keep our legacy alive.

Without passing down our history to our children, the legacy of Africa will once again be lost. Achievements are wonderful, but we all need a place to belong. For far too long, African Americans have hung in the balance, trying to be "just American" while wondering about the Africa that seems so foreign and distant. Draw near as I unwrap my Africa for you. May it be forever in your heart.

WINDOW TO AFRICA

Though Africa is faced with many things, there are still many beautiful places there, not unlike vacation spots in Jamaica and the Caribbean, areas where people flock to during traveling season. While some come to view the depressed areas and give aid, others choose to relax on Africa's beautiful beaches and nature retreats above any other place in the world. No one talks about this aspect of Africa very much in the media. Africa is not uncultured and full of heathens.

It is up to us to both discover and share the positive side of Africa with the world. Take it from me, it is grand. I know my Africa like the back of my hand. I know because Africa is me and she is beautiful. From picture-perfect vacation spots to bustling cities with high-rise buildings, Africa sparkles like a diamond at night in some places. There is more to Africa than the famine and disaster portrayed in the media, just as there is more to America than the music videos, commercials, and advertisements seen around the world. No matter where we are, everything that glitters isn't always gold. And yet African people know how to make the best of it. May the joy and perseverance of the African people be an inspiration to the entire world.

On my last visit back home, I saw beautiful people everywhere. Young teen girls who knew who they were and held their heads high as they walked along draped in bright cloth and cheery smiles. Young African boys were all over the marketplace with bright-eyes hopeful for the future and hands ready to work another day. The open market place for Africans is like walking the malls of America. You can find anything you want there. Indeed, I found what I wanted. Everywhere there were African men and women looking pleased and happy with themselves! Africa is full of entrepreneurs, people with small businesses and selling goods to others in the market place. Our minds are not idle.

To see photos of African cities, visit:
http://www.windowofafrica.com or
http://www.keletisanon.com.

CHAPTER FOUR

IT TAKES A VILLAGE: TRADITIONS OF RESPECT AND REARING

In 1996, Hilary Rodham Clinton wrote a book called *It Takes a Village* concerning the rearing of children. Regardless of their political persuasions, most Africans would say that's at least half-right—it takes a village ... and a family to raise a child.

In Africa, if anyone sees a child doing something wrong, they make it their business to correct the youth. They do this without any fear of conflict with the child's parents or the authorities. In America, if you chastise someone's child, you have committed a crime. A parent can even go to jail for spanking a child who is talking back if the child calls in and makes a report. It is hard for me to fathom a time in which a child back home would ever dare talk back in the first place, and they would definitely never call the authorities on their parents.

Nowadays, I hear about children cursing their parents out, beating them, and things I cannot imagine. This "time out" society has created teenagers who think they can do anything without any repercussions. While America is the Land of the Free, some children here may have too much freedom to express themselves.

Just because American kids are encouraged to be all they can be in life doesn't mean they get to act like fools whenever they want to. In Africa, there are limits and those limits are for the betterment of the child. Though America has many amazing structures and organizations, we could stand to adopt some of the African ideas of community regarding children.

The village concept of child rearing would also help young single mothers trying to do everything alone. In Africa, everyone in the city or in the village is responsible for the wellbeing of children. We recognize that children are valuable. They are our future, and they must have a firm grasp on respect for self and others. There is always someone minding the babies, and I don't mean a video game or TV set. Whether male or female, there needs to be a clearly identified head of household. Someone has to keep up with the kids or they will be lost.

ROLE OF THE OLDEST BROTHER

Though there are cultural differences across the vast continent of Africa, my experience with friends from different African countries is that we share a strong family foundation in common. For example, as the eldest son in my family, I was seen as the replacement for my father. It was a special position, but also a position of authority. The other brothers and sisters will always look to the elder brother for wisdom and support. Even when they are married, sisters often look to their elder brothers for help if they are in trouble. In the absence of the father, the eldest boy will be involved in many decisions for the family.

Children in my culture do not leave home at age eighteen. They may stay at home for as long as they like, as long as they are doing the right things, behaving well and participating in the traditions of the community. If the father dies, the eldest son will step up and take over the home.

Families in the part of Ivory Coast where I grew up often live in a compound. It's a big square, lined up with apartments for nine or ten families in a common area. Though some children might move out of their parents' family home, they often get an apartment in a compound nearby in the next neighborhood. Sometimes the parents of several children who grew up together or cousins get together and rent a house for the children. The parents will pay the rent until the young people get on their feet and find a job to pay.

Though the young people are on their own, they know that their oldest brother is the first one to call and he is the head of things behind their father. The older brother will talk to his siblings as much as possible, knowing that they will not take any steps further without him. Even once the family is in the US, many families continue this tradition, especially if the oldest brother is in America and the father is at home.

If a guy is paying attention to an unmarried sister, the woman must talk to her brothers and uncles, especially the oldest brother. After so many years here, I do not always cling to the strictest tradition, but I honor the respect paid me when someone asks my opinion. The family knows that sometimes a chain of command can be a protection, especially for a woman in today's world. Still, I trust the women in my life enough to release them from the tradition unless they insist.

In anything the older brother is asked, he must not rush to make an answer. All the men, fathers, brothers, and uncles, must meet and discuss things, especially something as critical as a potential husband for a female relative. "Give me some time" is a common response when a man in my culture is pressed for an answer.

Though a bride in my culture may be almost 30 years old, the men in the family need to know that she is stepping on good ground. How a man grew up is important. Though divorce is not as common in Africa as it is in America, the men of the family need to be sure that this is not a man who will divorce—and disgrace—their daughter or sister.

EDUCATION

Education is a huge deal in Africa, probably because it's not free like here in America. If a family doesn't have money to send their kids to school, the kids stay home. In America, this would be considered a horrible thing, but a child doesn't miss something he never did. When I was growing up, one of my friends would follow me to school and wait to play with me on break time. His parents couldn't pay for uniforms and fees.

Here in America, public school (K-12) is easy and free! School in Africa is so difficult, but I persevered because I saw others suffering and knew that it was a privilege to go to school. Where I am from, if you get to go to junior high, that is huge! If you get the high school diploma, this is a great accomplishment that cost lots of time and money. The parents can rejoice, knowing that this means the family will likely make it out of poverty. This also brings added respect to the family and to the parents for getting their child through their school courses.

If a child comes to America to go to school, now this is something everyone respects. Once, when I was at home in Ivory Coast and a man found out that I had graduated several times in America, I was escorted to meet a high ranking government official! The problem is that there aren't many jobs in my country for those who complete their education. Though Ivory Coast is no longer a French colony, there is still a great deal of French influence and a high school graduate from France can come to Ivory Coast and get a job as a teacher and get a free car, a villa to live in, and a good salary. This is still going on today. The French teachers go home on holiday to Paris while the African studies only to find that there are no jobs. However, every African country knows that a powerful country can afford to arm a militia to overthrow your government if you don't go along with what they want, and so, we go along.

If you listen to the stories about Africa's state of being, you will no doubt walk away believing that Africa does not have a working educational system in place, or that our schools are just for the privileged. But this is not true. We have primary, secondary and universities from one end of Africa to the other. Most Africans can read, write, and speak several different languages. Our learning institutions benefit us. They may not be lavish buildings with all the modern advantages that the schools have in America, but the focus is always on education. We have doctors, lawyers, engineers, teachers, artists, sports players, and musicians; all coming out of Africa.

African teachers as well as students take education seriously. Students respect one another and the classroom. There is no disruption of the classroom with unruly behavior or special techniques to deal with behavioral problems. African students know what is expected of them and so they act accordingly for the majority.

If you are parent of a school age child, continue to teach your child to respect teachers and other students, despite how other children may behave. If you are a teacher of African-American children, continue to challenge them at the highest levels, even if they have been taught to do the minimum amount of work. Their African heritage is one of strength, intelligence, and hard work.

CRIME

In America, if someone starts running and they stole something, the people watching will call the police. In Africa, if a guy starts running and he stole something, everybody comes out of their houses and chases the guy. They start beating him before the police come! It's tough to be a thief in Africa. After the beating, you will go to jail. One month or so later, you might be released. Even children will be chased if they steal something. I remember once some boy took a man's radio and went up on the roof. People were throwing rocks up at the boy until he came down. Even I was taken to the jail once for getting on the city bus without a pass. I was never so glad to see my parents.

In Ivory Coast, there is violence in many places, but if you call the police, you'd better be sure that what you're saying is really going on. If not, the police officer might punish you instead of the person you called the police about.

RESPECT FOR ELDERS

One thing that I hope never dies in Africa is the practice of respecting elders. Even here in America, it used to be that if an older person was standing on the bus, a young man or woman would get up and offer the elder a seat. A man would offer a seat to a woman also, rather than have her stand. Not so anymore.

In America, I have seen a woman eight months pregnant riding standing up for several miles on a crowded city bus on her way to the doctor. Without me offering her my seat, she probably would have had to go into labor to sit down. These silly people just kept looking up at her, smiling and asking when the baby was due.

In my country, that would be rude and unacceptable. Where is the respect in something like that? The children in my village are taught as soon as they can walk and talk to respect their elders. The entire village plays a part in making sure that the values taught at home are carried out in the community.

Another amazing thing here in America is the number of nursing homes with a community of elderly people being taken care of by nurses. I understand that people get sick and need to be cared for, but I don't understand how so many children can put their parents in a facility and not even visit them. How can people become so busy that they cannot even check on their elderly parents?

In Africa, the idea of putting one's parents in a home to be taken care of by strangers is nearly unheard of. We don't sign them up for assisted living or retirement communities. It is an African tradition that we as adult children give back to our parents by caring for them when they are up in age and cannot do for themselves. We take care of all their needs so they don't have to worry about being a burden or intruding. It is our privilege to care for them.

Even if we leave Africa to study or work abroad, we will take care of our parents. We send them money out of our paychecks, even if they don't need it, because it is an obligation. It is a tradition that we honor without making a big deal of it. Not so in America. The family structure here has weakened, and both young children and elderly parents are left to fend for themselves and rely on the system.

Today's children seem to be sitting around, waiting for the expiration date to arrive so they can collect what their parents left them. After a funeral of a parent, it's even worse: snatching, grabbing, feuding, and fighting over possessions and money seems to be the norm.

In my experience, this type of disrespectful behavior toward a deceased parent doesn't exist in Africa. We respect and care for our loved ones before and after death. This is a tradition we hold on to and pass on to our offspring because you never want to leave your elderly parents in need.

If this concept is new to you and your parent(s) are still alive, consider taking $20, $30 or $100 (whatever you can afford) and just giving it to your parent without them asking you for help. Most people will say they must wait until they make more money, but if you really want to do something, you will do it, even if it is for a very small amount. Whatever you give, know that God will triple your efforts. Please love your parents and stand by them, sharing with them as you can. This is how we are taught in Africa and this is how we do things. It is in this same way that each of us was able to get to America, go to school or do something. Someone gave to help us.

RESPECT FOR SELF

While respect for elders is very important in African culture, respect for self is important as well. The Bible says, "As a man thinketh in his heart, so is he" (Proverbs 23:7, KJV). The Bible also talks about the power of words. If there is one thing in African-American culture that absolutely stupefies me, it would be some of the derogatory language that African-Americans use to refer to themselves, such as *nigger* and *bitch*.

Nigger is defined in the American Heritage Dictionary as "a person of any race or origin regarded as contemptible, inferior, and ignorant."[29] One definition goes on to add that only a black person can refer to another black person this way and not be offensive. Not so. No matter who says it, this word is as degrading as it was when the slave masters used it on the plantations. Just because you dare someone who is not of your race than skin tone to say it, doesn't make it acceptable for intelligent, loving African people to say to one another.

---

[29] "nigger." *The American Heritage® Dictionary of the English Language, Fourth Edition.* Houghton Mifflin Company. 2004. 22 Jun. 2009
<http://dictionary.reference.com/browse/nigger>.

Just like the shackles that were removed from our ankles, this demeaning term needs to be removed from the African-American vocabulary. Like baggy sloppy jeans worn below the buttocks like prisoners denied a belt, this word and others like it pull us down lower and lower every time it is spoken.

If we want people to see a positive image of us, we must change what flows from our mouths. Not all African-Americans are comedians. Our history is not a comic strip where words used for centuries to degrade can now be adopted as terms of endearment. This is confusing, both to our young people and to the world. Instead, let's go back to "cousin" or "brother." At least these words signify some positive connection.

That brings me to something else that perplexes me, the lack of respect shown to black women. African-American women aren't bitches as they are often referred to in much of today's hip hop lyrics. Worse yet, our beautiful daughters and sisters are beginning to accept this nasty term and use it themselves! A bitch is a female dog, walking on four legs. This is no way to describe the black woman, a symbol of strength and courage the world over. We must stop saying this, women and men alike.

We must respect ourselves and our families by choosing better words to denote love and respect. If we do not, we cannot be angry when other cultures refuse to refer to us with words other than those of our own choosing. If a four-year-old girl says she wants to grow up to be a bitch instead of a doctor or a lawyer, what would we say? What could we say? We must speak a new destiny with principles from an old culture.

Nowhere in my country does this type of demeaning cultural behavior exist among people. Only in America is the way and words of slavery being brought back on ourselves by ourselves as if once were not enough. Martin Luther King, Jr. said, "We will overcome." Many think that with the election of President Barack Obama, black people in America have triumphed. While it is a great thing that has happened, sometimes I wonder if this generation isn't flip-flopping and going backwards.

We must hold fast to who we are and respect ourselves and our fellow man regardless of what is going on around us. Everywhere you go, everything you say, consider whether it will leave a positive impression of your family. Respect doesn't come from the pages of a textbook or even from the streets. It starts at home, in the heart of a child, so that we can grow up to speak and relate to others with consideration and understanding.

VILLAGE LIFE

As we've said, the responsibility of raising children doesn't lie with the parents alone. Everyone in the African village or compound takes a role in the raising of a child. This helps cultivate the responsibility required to become a productive member of society.

Even if a child's parents die, he or she will not be without instruction. The community will all take on the responsibility of nurture and provision. It is a great blessing to an African to take care of those who cannot care for themselves.

In America, it is possible to live next door to someone and never truly know them. People rush to their cars, to the jobs and back home again, rarely looking up to see who is around them in the neighborhood. In Africa, there is no such thing as not knowing your neighbor. Your community is your family and everyone knows each other. Everyone attends weddings, funerals, birth celebrations, and graduations. When Africans come to America, this is something that many of them miss.

The media convinces the world that Africans are uncivilized, but after witnessing the behavior of American youth in public places, I sometimes wonder which nation is really the uncivilized one. The type of rebellion, loud talk, and lewd behavior I have seen would never be tolerated in Africa. Young people there know that they must always exhibit good character or they will bring shame on their families and communities. An African knows this and seeks to represent his family and people well. All African Americans must start with their own families and create an atmosphere of love and respect in their homes.

CHAPTER FIVE

Food and Family:
The Ivorian Home

One can hardly have a discussion about Africa without mentioning food. Food, or the lack of it, is usually the first thing mentioned when Africa is in the media. In truth, poverty is a problem in Africa, but not everyone is starving. We enjoy eating together and cook simply and efficiently so that we are always able to share. In a society where every corner lures us with fast food drive-thru windows, all Americans can learn something from the thrift and nutrition of the food served in my country.

In America, there are so many choices for what to eat that people stand in the grocery store wondering what to buy. In Africa, meals are centered around the one item in every house—a 50 pound bag of rice. For some families, the rice bag is the easiest way to save money. In Ivory Coast, one American dollar is worth 500 francs. For $20 American, the wife can get a 50 pound bag of rice which can last more than a month for a family of six or seven. It is better to buy in bulk this way because there will always be something to eat.

BREAKFAST

Many Mandingo people start the day with a breakfast of rice pudding. In the homes of those rich families with big screen TVs, air conditioning, security guards, and gates, there will be bread, butter, eggs, and bacon. For unmarried guys with money, they can go to the kiosk and get scrambled eggs, sausage, bread, and butter with coffee for less than 50 cents.

Most neighborhoods have a kiosk with an umbrella on top. It's like a small coffee shop serving all kinds of breakfast. The man at the kiosk cooks fast and good. Your meal will be ready in less than ten minutes. Breakfast is from around 6:00-8:30 AM. Parents will not send their children off for school until they have had breakfast. In a compound, there may be several groups of children eating together before they go off to school.

LUNCH

The midday meal in my family was usually something to swim in. Lots of wet food and of course, a lot of rice! There would likely be a big pot of soup full of beef cubes, oil, onions, beef, and tomato paste. The Mandingo wife will pour water over this and let it cook for hours while she makes the rice. Once the rice is ready, she will put the rice in a big bowl and the soup in another bowl. She will put her husband and children on one side of the table, knowing that people can pop up whenever they choose to visit, and she must feed whoever chooses to join them.

If someone shows up, the mother will bring out whatever she has on reserve for the afternoon. She may save the rice for dinner and cook another meat gravy soup to go with it. The meat alone is a big deal. You don't eat the meat until your father gives it to you. In most Mandingo homes, the family will circle around the father during meals, symbolizing his role as leader of the home. Lunch is between noon and around 1 PM.

DINNER

Our final meal is very similar to lunch, only larger in quantity. Dinner is from around 6 to 7 PM. As soon as the children have left for school each day, the wife will go to the market to get fresh foods or condiments to cook. The market is usually two to three miles away. If the wife is pregnant, then another woman or the daughter of the house might go and get things from the market though most African women will try to go to the market herself until the very end. It's good for the labor and for the baby. However, it's not very safe for the wife at the market if she is pregnant and her stomach gets bumped by all the people, so she has to be careful.

Having been satisfied with a simple menu for most of my life, it was a shock to come to America and see a McDonald's on every corner. At first I compared every dime I spent here to its equivalent African money. I would say, "Oh no. This is too much money. I want that hamburger, but I can't spend that much money. I'm not going to do this." Eventually I remembered that this was not Africa, and I broke down and tried some things.

Of course, there was a curiosity to taste everything at first, while still comparing price. Some Africans take longer to give in than I did, passing up the golden arches for another 50 pound bag of rice. It's hard to eat three dollars' worth of French fries when you are thinking about whom might need that money back at home. The day comes though when the newcomer has no choice but to go and buy something.

Hamburgers! Fried chicken! At first I went crazy. For some, it may take as long as a year to slow down on the American food and want African food again. Eventually I began to gain weight while my wallet got slimmer. In Africa, a person might walk 10-20 miles a day without realizing it. In the US, there is a lazy life with lots of food all the time and stress and driving. At home, there are people everywhere and I used to enjoy the walking. My eyes didn't measure how far my feet were going. Some rode motorcycles and bikes, but that was another step up in money. It was also dangerous with so many people trying to walk around you. It is interesting in America to see so many people driving to the store to buy more food only to rush home and try to walk some of it off.

After a while, the longing for African food returned. Though I eat some American food sometimes, it is hard for most Africans to go days without some form of African food or at least Spanish, Jamaican or Caribbean food. If these are available, many Africans will eat them before fast food.

CHAPTER SIX

A FAMILY AFFAIR: AFRICAN CELEBRATIONS AND CULTURE

While in America, matters of the heart are decided by a man and woman alone, in Africa, marriage is a family affair. It isn't just the joining of two people, but two families. Once the bond is made, it cannot be easily broken. The same family members who agree to bring two people together would also have to consent to tear them apart. Though people come to the West and adopt different views, the African marriage is to be for life.

DATING

People often ask me about how dating works at home. The answer is easy. In the culture I grew up in, there was no dating! You read it right. No dating. You get married. It was that simple. It was more like courting if anything. You could like someone, but you could not touch them unless you married them. You could not be seen in public "hanging out," "chilling," or "just talking."

Though modern culture and media has brought the concept of dating to Africa, most parents are still against it. There are still ladies in my country up to age 25 who are free to go anywhere but will not date. They are afraid of being caught with a man and bringing shame on their family. These girls want to be married honorably according to Mandingo tradition. However, it is my belief that you must live in the society you find yourself in. I am now an African-*American*. Many African fathers would not allow their daughters to bring a boyfriend home back in Africa, but they allow it here so that their girls can bring home a husband.

MARRIAGE

Marriage in African-American society today differs from marriage in Africa. According to the Administration for Children and Families, 68% of African-American births were to unmarried women in 2003 and 62% of African-American households were led by a single parent in the same year. Forty-one percent of African-American adults are married; however, they just don't seem to be having any children![30] There is also a high divorce rate in the African-American community. In Africa, marriage is viewed as a joining of families to create a family, and it is taken very seriously.

American women, both black and white, begin dreaming about their wedding day from the time they hear their first fairytale. They spend the rest of their lives looking for Prince Charming, often while passing over good men all around them.

---

[30] AAHMI. "African American Healthy Marriage Initiative." Administration for Children and Families. 26 Jun. 2009
<http://www.acf.hhs.gov/healthymarriage/about/aami_marriage_statistics.htm>.

Real life and real love doesn't always mean happily ever after, but it can mean a good life and a beautiful family.

This is hard to swallow for a woman who has spent her childhood dreaming about her wedding day and a year or more spending money she doesn't have on the perfect dress and dream location. Two years later, however, when the reality of married life sets in, she may be headed for a divorce lawyer.

If a couple doesn't give the marriage union a chance to blossom and grow, they will never know the joys of a good marriage. While there are many older couples who celebrate being married up to 30, 40 and 50 years, today's brides and grooms are likely to throw in the towel when the first obstacles arise. Perhaps this is because the support needed to sustain a marriage isn't always there.

All over the world, the family is under attack. We must all go back to our beginnings and try to provide a family foundation that will withstand the times. The African marriage provides a good model by uniting not only the couple as man and wife, but bringing together two families for life as well. Perhaps if couples see themselves as joining the community as one family instead of just two individuals, things will improve.

In my country, the connection between families starts long before the wedding day. Families are very involved in the marriage of their son or daughter, not to meddle in their relationships, but to support them and prepare them to enter a lifelong union.

In America, people take their marriage problems to strangers, paying money to counselors for help. In Africa, the same family members who witnessed the wedding are the ones who share wisdom and help the couple work through problems.

The character of both families will be reviewed and recommendations given on whether this is a good family to be joined to.

Not only will the families be under consideration, but the bride and groom themselves. Are they mentally and emotionally stable enough for marriage? The family and community will observe their attitudes and actions before making a judgment on this. If there is bad behavior on the part of either bride or groom, the actions of the young person will shame their family, and their parents will be held accountable. There is no running off to Vegas or going to the Justice of the Peace. The African wedding tradition involves both sides of the family and is carried out in a thoughtful, serious way.

That said, marriage in Africa is not perfect either. There are still many cultures where a man can have more than one wife and girls are married off by their parents at a young age. In America, men have more than one wife; they just don't legally marry their mistresses and outside girlfriends. Young girls here are not married off by their parents but often are sexually active and living with or in relationships with men much older them, who might as well be their husbands. A stronger commitment to marriage as a sacred institution can help change these things.

For those not yet married, consider adding more African flair to your union than just jumping the broom at the ceremony. Consider getting both families involved in the entire marriage process and holding yourself accountable to them throughout your married life. It might make a difference when temptation or trouble comes if there is more at stake than your own individual happiness.

THE MARRIAGE PROPOSAL

In our culture, marriage is not taken lightly. Once you involve all the people it takes—men and women—to bring together a couple, you cannot easily break that bond. Both families are now joined to each other, fused by the marriage they agreed to. To break that bond, the couple will need the permission of all the people they brought together through their union, especially the older people. There is no way out without shaming everyone, including yourself.

When a man sees a lady he is interested in, he will not try to stop her on the street or get her attention. If he does, she will quickly tell him that he must talk to her father and get away so that no one thinks badly of her. If the young man is honorable, he will go and tell his people who the girl is and that he wants to marry her. The boy's family will try to find out who the girl's family is and if these are good people. If all the elders of the family agree, an on-go-ye (a messenger) will be sent to present some news to the father that this family would like to meet.

When the messenger comes to the house, the mother will offer the person a place to sit down and give them water. They must accept this as it a welcome to the home. The mother will go and call the father, who will listen to the person's introduction of the young man.

The oldest boy will come and also hear the news and listen to his father's instructions on how to go and spread the news to the father's younger brothers and closest relatives. The oldest son must represent the history and tradition of the family. Once the sisters are married, they belong to their husband's family. If the couple has problems, the husband will send a message to the wife's family, usually the older brother or the lady's mother, saying that his wife would like to come home and visit. Only then can she come back to her family of birth and spend the night. Though she may visit every day, every night she will go home to her husband unless he has requested that she come home for a time. Both families took the commitment of marriage and agreed that God gave the woman to the man. If she wants to stay overnight, even in the home of her parents, she must talk to her husband.

Compared to relationships in America, this might sound formal, but we're not talking about a rich family here. Rather, this would be the way a poor family rich in integrity would conduct things. This is the way of a family who lives in a compound, but is working hard to pay for their children's school fees, trying to get ahead. They will one day try to buy their own land and if their kids grow up, they will want to get their children a driver's license or training so that they can make money if there aren't any jobs. This type of family will always try to upgrade their lifestyle and see having a large family as part of that. They think that if they have a lot of kids, then one of them might actually make it and take care of them.

The wedding messenger that is sent to the woman's father will be well spoken and if possible, well known by the girl's mother's side of the family. The father will listen and accept the messenger's gift of kola nut, a traditional way of accepting the union in Mandingo culture. However, he will not consent to the wedding right away. The father will tell the messenger to come back in two or three days. He will then call all elders of the family—or have his oldest son call them—brothers, sisters, the girl's uncles mother's side's relatives, etc. When the messenger returns, he will still have the kola, but he won't come alone. Someone from the family, perhaps even the man himself will come with him.

"Such and such family is interested in your daughter..." the messenger will say convincingly, trying to sell the brother to the family while not pushing the truth too hard. Every message the man gives puts his own reputation on the line. If the man turns out to be no good, he has been part of bringing two people together for a lifetime and failed at it. He will give some background about the boy's family, saying things like they are stable, quiet people who stay out of trouble and have raised their family well. Again, the father of the bride will usually not accept the kola nut himself. He will likely let his younger brother or the messenger himself accept the kola and give the man's family another appointment in a week or so to come back.

It is time now for the mother of the bride's side of the family to sit down and call the daughter in and talk to her. This will go on for at least one day, but it could last for two days or more. "This guy says he wants to marry you. Do you want to marry him? Are you sure you like this guy? Do you want him or don't you?" The bride-to-be will answer the same questions again and again, showing just enough enthusiasm to let the family know that she wants to marry the man but not with too much happiness or they will think something improper has been going on.

The aunts, sisters and mother will try to evaluate the man, his character, how his family is, whether they have been in trouble, how often they've been hearing bad things about this family and so on. They are here to help the girl make up her mind, but in the end, it is her choice. No one will force her to get married, but if she agrees to do it, then she must understand the commitment that she is making.

Eventually, the mother-of-the-bride's family will be satisfied and the girl's mother will go and talk to the girl's father about what has been decided. Sometimes they will overrule the girls' decision if the family is known to be too much trouble. About three days before the messenger is to return for the next appointment, the mother of the bride will call everyone on her side of the family to come over again. They will form a circle around the daughter, men on one side and women on the other side.

At this point, the uncle will openly ask the bride-to-be one final time if she wants to marry this man. "This is your day to speak. Today is the day to tell us whether you want this or don't want it because tomorrow they are going to be coming. If you accept this, then we all will accept their kola and the ceremony will proceed. If not, we will return their kola and let them go home."

At this point, the woman still has the right to say yes or no. If she says that she wants him and the whole family is there, some who weren't present before will ask more questions. "Do you know this man? What kind of contact have you been having with him? Has everything been decent and in order between the two of you?"

The girl will explain. "Yes, we have talked briefly. He said hello and expressed interest in me and I told him to come and see my family. This is why he sent the messenger." The family will accept this and ask everyone there if they know anything that is against this guy she is about to marry. The families are

A FAMILY AFFAIR

going to become one now. They want to be sure that they will not regret this decision one day down the road. Again they will ask her, one last time, "Are you sure?" At this point, every relative in the compound will arrive to give their input, even children! Other families in the compound are quiet and listening for sounds of celebration. Everyone knows that soon a wedding is coming.

The next day, when the messenger arrives, all of the bride's extended family will be sitting down with the bride's mother and the messenger to say yes, go ahead and schedule the wedding. Now the messenger is relieved and very happy. He will go now and tell the other family to prepare to come and visit and they will start preparations for the wedding. Now the man's family and his family's elders will come and visit. The girl's family does not travel! If you want someone's daughter, you must go to them. They will come soon to express thanks. They will prepare food and bring it to the girl's family.

Now the girl's father must go to each door in his compound and announce the news to the head of each family that he has accepted an offer to marry his daughter to such and such family in such and such neighborhood. He will invite the man's family over so that he can introduce him to the compound. This can go on for as long as two or three hours. The messenger will be there. At this point they will announce when the wedding will be, usually within the next month.

The woman's side of the family will ask for things they need for the woman: a hope chest or dowry, clothes, gold jewelry, dishes, etc. In Africa, the amount of love the man has for a woman is measured by how much stuff he buys for his future wife. That part is not so much different from America!

The groom probably started buying things from the day he set eyes on the girl and knew that he wanted to marry her.

In big cities, longer engagements of a year or more are common after the Western style, but the village tradition is to do a ceremony sooner, but the man must be able to afford all the things the girl's mother says she will need. He must also be able to support her. Some men will go all around the city to find work so that they can get money to marry the girl they want. The girl may be as young as twelve years old, but he will go and work until she 17 or 18, knowing it will take him a while to afford everything.

THE MARRIAGE CEREMONY

The wedding is a big deal. There will be a traditional tam tam drum and a musician will be called to play. Some families have a quiet wedding because they don't have the money for the musician. Sometimes they don't have the money, but the extended family will pitch in to help them have a nice wedding. In more modern weddings, you will see a white dress, black tuxedo and shiny limousine. This is usually for couples whose parents are rich. They have a Mercedes for the couple to drive and hire a bus to carry all the people coming to the wedding across town to the event. This modern type of couple stands up in front of a church, records videotape to put on the Internet, has a big reception and a very classic and beautiful ceremony comparable to what you might see in the US. There could be anywhere from one hundred to over two hundred people at a wedding like this, followed by an elaborate honeymoon.

Back in the village, the bride has long been married while the city girl was ordering flowers. Before she gets married though, the village bride will go to a special counseling for three days with three elder women in her family. The Mandingo tradition especially likes to do this. This will be a deep and special counseling time with the women from her mother's and father's sides of the family. They are going to talk to her about how she should behave when she gets married and I mean everything! She will hear her mothers and aunties explain how to talk to her husband, how to behave, how to deal with trouble. She may learn secrets as part of this education that she never imagined. She must stay with the women until the three days are over. Then, she will leave the three elder ladies and go straight to the wedding party. She will have something covering her face like a scarf. The older ladies will pull it up and present her to the groom and all the people attending. She is now a wife! At this moment, everyone is jumping, dancing and filled with joy.

Whether the bride is from the village or the city, all weddings will have a certain structured chaos. People will be traveling and dancing and coming together. Later that day when the wedding is over, a traditional drum player will be chosen to beat the tam tam drum and lead the girl to her husband's house. They will have another ceremony to receive her into the new family in a few days, but for now, the newlyweds will be left alone.

In the meantime, the two families are now joined. The two mothers-in-law will walk to the market together. They will cook and share food. The younger siblings now have a new place to go—their sister's compound. This will also give them a new group of friends.

THE CHILDBIRTH BLESSING

In my own country, Ivory Coast, there are about 60 different ethnic groups, each with different ways of celebrating certain ceremonies. In my Mandingo tribe, the most common celebration for newborns is that after the woman is home from the hospital in the city, she and her baby will be taken care of by her other relatives and neighbors from her compound. All family and friends will come to welcome the mom and baby, praying for good health and prosperity for the family. Meanwhile, it is the husband's responsibility to announce the birth of his child to everyone.

The father and his messenger will go around and announce the news of the birth and when the baby naming celebration will be. He will usually do this on the same day the child is born, but definitely within seven days of the birth, usually on a Sunday because most people are off work, including students. The ceremony will be on the closest Sunday to the birth so that no one will miss work and children will be able to attend, too. The family will make sure that the birth is announced to all, even people across town. Sometimes their news will even arrive in the next village. The village people are not forced to make the trip, but sometimes they will come when news is announced depending on who and what it is. Most often they will come only for the death of a close relative.

During the first week of the child's life, many visitors will stop by to see the baby and pray for the baby before the main event. Before the ceremony, the father will buy a live chip (lamb) or a cow to be killed for the ceremony. The meat will be distributed to all the people who come to the ceremony.

Some other form of snack will be given also to take home with them. The ceremony is held in the morning, from around 7 AM to 10 AM.

The morning of the ceremony, everyone will arrive dressed very clean. There will easily be 30 or more people, women in the room with the mother and most men sitting chairs in a big circle in the compound. By this time, the father and mother have already decided on the name of their child. Someone will have been chosen in advance to guide the ceremony and that person will announce the opening of the event by asking for everyone's attention and then praying for the baby and mother. After a time of praying, the person guiding the ceremony will ask a group of elders to pray. They will send more prayers the baby's way as well as the family.

Finally, one of the elders will take the baby in his hand and in a low voice, say the baby's name seven times in each ear, starting with the right side. After that, the person guiding the ceremony will officially announce the baby's name to everyone. He will speak very loudly, saying, "The baby's name is…" He will repeat it several times.

At this point, everyone now knows the baby's name and will be praying for the baby one more time, saying "God bless baby _____, his mother, father and family, and may God bless all of us and the time we have here together."

The elder men will now kill the cow or lamb and a few younger people will help process and make many packets of meat so that everyone that came can take some meat to their home and cook.

At this point, the ceremony is over and most people will start to leave now. On their way out, they will go into the room with the mother and give her some gift: money, soap, clothes, etc. The family will designate some responsible kids to take some meat to other families in the neighborhood who stopped by earlier in the week but could not make it to the ceremony due to work or other personal situations.

FAMILY SIZE

In Mandingo culture, twins are viewed as a great honor, especially if they are boys. The more boys the family has, the better chance that the kids will stay around and help out since the girls go to their husband's family. This is a blessing.

The average village family doesn't have bills since Africa isn't a credit society like America. You get your land and then you build as you can. Once the family has land, they can also farm and expand the farm if the family grows. They might even have a small store. Some people will just have as many kids as they want in the village. It's open. The belief is that if God gives you a child, you just accept it.

Even in a compound, you may see big families, but as the kids do well, they will move out. A son may succeed and build his parents their own compound with a big house for them. Some will still stay where they are and tell the younger ones to go. Some older people do not want to leave their compound. They have spent their lives with their neighbors and they would be lonely.

In the city, it's different. People will have maybe two or three children and that's it. They live more like people in the US except that people still tend to live more together than in individual houses like here in America. If I'd grown up here, I think it might have been a lonely childhood. There was always someone to play with, always someplace to go. Everything in America is so serious: work, home, sleep, pay bills and then start over again.

People in the States leave their houses empty and shut the doors. This makes Africans miss home where people are welcoming you everywhere you go. When I am home, I enjoy every second. The American system of working and working can swallow people up. They are stressed with jobs, bills, mortgages. Often it's not just one job either, it's two. In Africa, there are no credit cards. You can have a debit card, no overdraw. Though we can get more here, I wonder sometimes if it isn't killing us and taking the joy away from our culture.

For some Africans, America is everything they dreamed. Others come here, get a credit card or two and go crazy. Everything is just given to them. They lose control. They did so well at home, but now no one is watching them. They can buy a car and a cell phone and this and that... They are trying to reach a level that is too high.

In Africa, every young man is trying to be American. He is watching the rappers and singers on American TV and they want to be them. They are dressing American and comparing themselves to African-Americans. They see the connections that some of us adults have missed and slide right in to the culture. For some, it is just a phase. For others, it can be a challenge for them and their families to adjust their expectations. To see what a large city in my country is like, visit

http://www.abidjan.net.
http://www.planetabidjan.com
http://www.ivoirebusiness.net
http://www.ivoirebusiness.net
http://www.abidjanshow.com
http://www.abidjanshow.com
http://www.cotedivoiremarriage.net
http://www.abidjantv.net
http://www.hotels.ci
http://www.africultures.com

THE AFRICAN ELDER

I have spoken some about the responsibility of the older brother. When my parents died, my father's brother took in my family though he already had two kids of his own. He was no longer my uncle; he was now my father. He paid for everything and gave us the chance to continue going to school. In Africa, the man's side pays for things if possible. I am encouraged to see this tradition continue in many American-born black families as well.

HEALTH CARE

Though it is easy to forget when standing in an American pharmacy, Africans know well that all medicine originates from a plant or tree. For thousands of years, Africans have cured themselves with living plants and trees. We know that all traditional medicine came from natural medicine and most pharmaceutical companies do their research in Third World countries before bringing their drugs to the most modernized countries in the west.

Third World countries have suffered the loss of a lot of knowledge that was once passed down for centuries due to secrets being stolen from corporations. Still, many people in Africa believe in natural medicine first, turning to modern medicine in a clinic or hospital only if natural treatment proves unsuccessful. Only those with stable jobs with health insurance benefits will be thinking about getting modern care as quickly as they can and taking a prescription to be filled at the pharmacy.

Most rural villages most likely rely on natural medicine as they have for centuries and will have a plant remedy for just about any common sickness in the region. In Ivory Coast, for example, and many other African countries, each village can report births to the closest town hospital. The town mayor and his team are responsible for informing all the chiefs of the villages of any new government rules and regulations concerning health care. Then the chief of each village will hold a general meeting, which everyone must attend, to inform of the new regulations.

Each town must have a modern hospital, which may be equipped with the most basic equipment to be able to respond to emergency. If the town hospital is not able to save someone's life, they will make a call to the capital city in order to evacuate the patient to that hospital. The city hospital may have a little advanced technology that might help save the person's life. The family of the patient will be responsible for most of the cost of the prescription drugs.

Middle class people will first think of the modern hospital when they are sick and proceed from there, much like here in the US. We do not have any form of welfare in my country like Medicare or Medicaid. Besides taking care of each other in the neighborhood, there is nothing to fall back on. If tragedy strikes and a situation become critical, we might ask the authority to help, but most of the time the help is very little. Because of this, health care is natural first and modern last. There is a lot of health insurance for those working in a high rise building in the city that have been to college and university and are working for a good company, but this is definitely for middle class or higher.

Though there can be problems with access to hospitals and doctors in Africa, natural medicine is still very strong and welcomed in most parts of Africa. I can remember as a child in the Mandingo tribe, from ages 6-12, my mother would boil leaves and roots from different trees and I would take a bath in the solution. Sometimes I would have to drink many full glasses of the solution. This was constant in my growing up years. Sometimes when people came to visit from the village, they would bring my mother other roots and leaves as a gift, and I would start the bathing and drinking process all over again. The idea behind my mother's preparations was to have a strong son, ready to meet any physical challenge or heavy duty job, a son who would never give up.

AIDS

AIDS is a big concern in Africa as I'm sure you know. All Africans are thankful to the US for all they have done in Africa concerning AIDS. While many do not agree with the politics of past president, George W. Bush, I have heard from people back at home that he did more for AIDS in Africa than anyone has ever done. Myself and all of Africa thank him for that and we will always remember him for that. Thanks to international funding from all over the world, there are AIDS awareness campaigns through TV, radio and newspapers and in schools and universities.

Communication is the main key to changing outcomes of AIDS in Africa. People aren't talking about AIDS openly like here in America. This silent killer needs to be taken very seriously and discussed openly among Africans. Governments are doing their part by sending awareness teams and agents into cities, towns and villages to tell people about the dangers of AIDS and the ways to protect themselves: condoms, abstinence, etc.

Another possible problem is the stigma concerning AIDS testing among Africans. For an African to take an AIDS test, it would be shameful to them. Many might think, "What if it's positive? Where will I find the resources to be cured and buy the prescriptions and drugs?" Some people think erroneously that it is better to not know. Here in the US, we see people who are HIV positive yet living good lives. The government health departments are working hard to help people get the courage to be tested and to understand the steps necessary for treatment if they are diagnosed HIV positive. These efforts are possible through funding from numerous international groups. There is an African-American religious charity that has been holding the Black Church Week of Prayer for the Healing of AIDS since 1998. Balm in Gilead, Inc. (http://www.BalminGilead.com) strives to improve the health status of people across the African Diaspora (everywhere the African slaves landed). They have a special focus on HIV/AIDS. They are just one of many organizations around the world seeking change concerning AIDS in Africa.

As Africans living in America, we need to do more in warning people back at home about the danger of not using protection during sex, not being tested for HIV and AIDS and not taking medication prescribed by a real licensed doctor. I personally wish sometimes that my people put a little more trust in the outside media when it comes to things like health issues and disease. Though I know that the media has depicted Africa in unflattering ways, there is always something new to be learned, especially concerning AIDS and the damage it is doing across the continent. This is one area where compromise with tradition and culture is necessary to save lives.

EDUCATION

In Africa, families are so happy to have their kids in school. The more the children advance in grades, the more the parents hope to be out of struggle soon and the more they look to a bright future. Again, when a child graduates high school, it is an honor to have sustained the 17 years of pressure to make it to university.

Most African countries have a similar educational setup to America with children going from first grade to twelfth grade. For general education, students study history, geography, science, mathematics, physical education, social sciences, grammar, French, English, and Spanish. At the university level, the student may choose his or her preference of study.

Young men at the university level are seen as heroes of the family. Their proud parents will constantly remind him to do better and help reduce their struggle. Those students who complete university and become a professional with a job are seen as a king or a queen. They are well respected and seen to be in the upper class and a leader, someone who is part of making and changing the modern world.

WELFARE

Though things might have changed while I have been in America, to my knowledge there is no place in Africa where the government is handing out financial assistance to its citizens. Government assistance as it exists in America is unheard of there. It is not necessarily a wrong concept, but the lack of it has forced Africans to be self-sufficient.

Throughout Africa, the majority of people are entrepreneurs in some capacity. Some have a little business of selling some wares or goods that they have made or grown. A visit to an African market shows instantly the number of independent, proud people making a living for themselves and their families. Even children can be seen helping out. In Africa, this is a respected thing, but in America and other developed countries, it is looked down upon, perhaps because these societies are based on big companies getting rich instead of individuals and small businesses flourishing.

Though Africa is considered a poor continent, we have dignity and pride, and our individual cultures make us proud to be African. Our richness cannot always be seen in terms of dollars, but if you look into our eyes and see our souls, one will view something priceless.

TECHNOLOGY

Technology is advancing in Africa like never before. In previous times, only the residents of cities could really use cell phones, cable or wireless, but today people in many villages are able to watch TV, use cell phones to call their family members in the city instead of taking a trip to announce news. Africans welcome technology and always want to include it in education and teach their children how to use it.

Though some think all Africans are behind the times, I must tell you that many people are walking around the village talking on a cell phone and watching the same TV shows as Americans before going to bed!

CHAPTER SEVEN

COMING TO AMERICA

It used to be that every man in Ivory Coast wanted to someday go to Paris. Though my country declared independence in 1960, we were all taught to see Paris as heaven on earth and France as the place of our language. I would imagine that England was viewed the same way for men from Ghana or Nigeria.

Once an African gets to France though, he might be surprised. Paris is crowded. There isn't enough housing. The hotel bedrooms are tiny, yet expensive. The most unexpected thing is that Africans are not really welcomed. Over 100 million French-speaking African citizens desire to go to France. However, there is no dual citizenship between France and their former colonies in Africa, despite the dual citizenship and favor allowed to many French people in post-colonial Africa. Africans are required to obtain a visa. Every year, residents of Benin, Burkina Faso, Burundi, Cameroon, Central African Republic, Chad, my own Cote d'Ivoire, Democratic Republic of Congo, Djibouti, Gabon, Guinea, Madagascar, Mali, Niger, Rwanda, Senegal, Togo, and other African countries apply for French visas. Many of them are denied. While it is all right for the colonizing country to establish villas and summer homes in the beautiful African country they once controlled, large numbers of French-speaking Africans on the streets of Paris are not wanted. And so, the dream of the Ivorian begins to change. No longer is France and Paris the object of his fantasy. His dream is now…America.

Once a person has an American visa, their family will have several meetings with their child leading right up until the day the child leaves. Everyone is most likely invited to counsel the person about good behavior: uncles, sisters, brothers, aunties, and neighborhood friends. Often, there will be a big party celebrating the departure of someone from the neighborhood going to America.

In the family's compound, the person going to America is seen as going close to heaven and improving their life's condition. The person leaving is envied by others who wish they were in your shoes. On the flip side, the responsibility is huge. You know the struggle people have at home and how many people had to help to get your US visa. By leaving Africa for America, all the expectation and trust of your whole family is placed in you. Finally now they will be able to stop struggling day by day as you improve to the next level. The responsibility is great, but at the same time it is a great motivation to succeed.

Though many Africans would agree that it takes a village to raise a child, they would also agree that the same child has the ability to save the village, or at least his family. In America, we are used to seeing change come through the government or some type of program. In Africa, change comes through the family. One person makes it and then he or she helps others, who help others and so on.

Though it will take a lot of self-control, self-discipline, determination, focus, ambition, and belief in God, one person can change the destiny of an entire family. If the person remembers every second where he came from and how many people are hanging on mentally and physically, hoping for him to make it, the African young person can make a change.

To do this, the newcomer must remember his people and stay focused, no matter how many distractions come his way. He must stay away from breaking laws. He must make friends with good people trying to do the same as him and set goals to pay the way for another family member—brother, sister, cousin—to join him in America so that he will be able to send more help back home.

Once that is achieved, he must keep bringing more family members or if permitted, send enough money so some family member can start some form of business to help the family improve locally in Africa. As the family situation gets better and more family comes to America, each one can be doing some form of trade and lighten the stress on the original family member who came to America first.

COMING TO AMERICA

Unlike the funny Eddie Murphy movie, *Coming to America*, the American dream can seem like a nightmare if you arrive in a country and find everything foreign—including yourself. While today there are many opportunities for study visas and programs, many immigrants have come to the country illegally. When I arrived in America, there were programs where Africans could work on a farm and get a work permit. Some Africans had enough money to pay for their permits without working. Others did not. From sun up to sun down, they would work for 90 days to get a chance to change their lives and the lives of their families back at home—a chance to spend five years in America and then pursue citizenship.

When I came here, I worked at many jobs including a car wash for $3 an hour. During this time, I could not leave the country or I would not have been able to return. Later, I filed for my work permit, and then became a temporary resident. Eventually, I became a permanent resident, and finally an American citizen.

AFRICAN-AMERICAN RELATIONS

When I came to the US, I was very scared of my whole situation, not knowing anyone here. On top of that, I looked at African Americans like geniuses, people black like me with a very advanced knowledge, perhaps more than any blacks on earth. These were the people that everyone at home wanted to be like, from politicians to musicians, athletes and dancers. These people seemed to have the blessing of God and be a step closer to God than anyone else. I was very scared of them and didn't know what to think at first.

There was also the fear of spending too much time with African Americans and losing touch with my African culture. For this reason, an African will want to stay in touch with any African from his country just to preserve the culture he is used to. The common culture of America can be a brutal change in a different direction from all one has known, especially in regards to loyalty and responsibility to family. I was concerned that I didn't do anything to dissolve my ambition and make me forget my people back home. I'd heard about the people who'd become like lost kids in America, floundering with no culture. One of the first things an African can become aware of in talking to African Americans is the impact of slavery on America. American slaves were beaten by slave masters for speaking their language, sold away from people from their same village or tribe, and left with little of their heritage. Slaves that were brought to the Caribbean and South America were allowed to retain much more of their culture, and so many Africans feel a strong kinship with people from these areas as they can look and see some part of African culture in their practices.

However, though we do not see a lot of Africa in some of today's African Americans, we are very proud of all they have accomplished. During slavery we lost millions of strong, intelligent people. Though the system of slavery sought to destroy all aspects of African culture, we are proud of the way African Americans survived despite this. If one looks closely, there is still Africa in the food, music and culture of African-Americans especially among the Gullah people of South Carolina.

In school in Africa, we even watch *Roots*, the TV series about slavery. When I saw it, the title was translated into French as *Racine*. Many people in Africa have let go of the idea of slavery and all the pain it caused on both sides of the sea. We now view African Americans like the winners at long last, standing strong in freedom in the most advanced country in the world.

African kids copy after the style of African-American entertainers, celebrities, and athletes. I hope that all American black celebrities know that their influence extends around the world, especially to all the young men and women in Africa, who are always watching them.

Africans choose to look at where African Americans are now and where they can go. We are proud of our cousins and want them to try to focus on the positive just as we must do at home when there are wars, hunger, sickness, or any other trouble.

Ironically, though there can be some misunderstandings between Africans and African Americans, most non-black Americans seem to really respect African immigrants. They see us as very structured, focused, and determined to reach our goals, willing to do whatever it takes to make it. They see us sticking together and trying to stay out of trouble, trying to have a heart and send help home, and they are impressed by it.

Unfortunately, I think that sometimes African-American unity suffers from these comparisons. In a way, this is the same feeling from slavery that the black American is lazy or unproductive. While it is true that native Africans are not ashamed of the kind of job we must do when we get here and perform that job with honesty and integrity, we know that our African-American cousins are dedicated workers as well. We appreciate the acknowledgement of non-Blacks but try not to take their praise at the expense of our cousins.

One part of the gift of African culture that I want to share here is the African heritage of contentment: living within our means, saving extra for bad days and reaching out to others both here and at home in Africa who need help, and getting blessed in the end for thinking of others. This is the African mindset that many African Americans have used to achieve success.

One interesting thing about being an African immigrant is starting to have relationships with African-American women. My experience is that the African-American woman will let some things go without a big fuss as long as the bills are paid and things are peaceful. Their parents will not interfere with their daughter's married life. They believe that it is their marriage and they need to experience it for themselves. The mother usually only gives counsel when asked to do so.

Many Africans would love to be married to an African-American woman if she understands his responsibility to people back home that they have to look out for and the desire to bring other family members over to help. In any cross-cultural relationship, there will be differences of opinion and misunderstanding, but I think that these can be overcome with openness and honesty.

RELATIONS WITH OTHER AFRICANS

One of the most amazing things about being in America is the ability to be with Africans from countries other than your own. While I am sharing some of my Ivorian culture with you in this book, I often spend time with other Africans and learn about their cultures as well. In Africa, family is so important that someone would rarely travel too far from their homes unless they are trying to better themselves in some way.

In my case, I was fortunate because the first group of Africans I met from outside my country were from Mali and

Guinea. These two groups are Mandingo descendants and speak Mandingo very well as their first traditional dialect. There were three groups of people from three different countries (including my own), but we all spoke Mandingo. Our traditions were very similar, and it was as if we were all born in the same house.

I later met and became friends with people from Ghana, Nigeria, Kenya, and South Africa. This was also a great experience observing and understanding their culture, traditions, food, and ceremonies; however, I wonder if it would have been different if I hadn't met people who spoke my language first. That was a great situation that I fell right into.

In other cases, groups of newcomers to the country must be accepted by Africans from different beliefs and religions. Over time, some form of friction may start because of these differences and some Africans will politely move away from the community they are in when their situation is improved to join a group of Africans with more similar beliefs and behaviors.

As a newcomer to the US, not knowing anyone, an African is thankful to any fellow African who will take him in from the street, welcome him into their home and their people, feed him, and guide him until he starts to better his condition, make friends, and start to know where the other Africans from his country is in his community. Then he will build friendships with others as well as the people he is living with and even after he moves out to live with people from his own country or region, he will come back to visit from time to time to say thanks for what was done for him. This family will always be part of his extended African brotherhood in the US.

Another thing that happens is that people from different African countries might marry each other. I did that. I was married to a lady from Gabon in Central Africa. There were some cultural differences regarding the husband's responsibility to do the same in the wife's country as he does in his own as far as buying land and building houses, family having say in the marriage and so on. Due to these differences, I did all I could for the family to visit often and for my wife to visit them.

The food from her country was very different but good. I did visit Gabon a couple times, and I observed that most people there have a husband or wife from the same country. The Gabonese really don't believe in marrying Africans from other countries, but sometimes they do. In some cases, men or women have taken the children back to their original country without anyone knowing and never come back, so many think it is best to just marry someone from your own country. Many other African countries have the same feelings about marrying their own people.

In Gabon, all Africans from other African countries must pay a yearly fee of close to $800 US for their resident card to live there, maybe more than that for a family. All citizens from countries other than Gabon are called foreigners and must pay a fee. Gabon is a small country, but it is very prosperous with oil and has a strong national pride.

JOBS IN AMERICA

When Africans first arrive, African restaurants are a decent job, but temporary. The newcomer or Africans without a resident card will take anything until things get better, but if the owner wants a legal restaurant with legal papers, he has to be careful about the people he hires. One good thing about working at a restaurant is that lots of Africans from all parts of Africa might come and eat there. You will be more comfortable as a newcomer to see people socialize like in Africa, and there will also be people sharing information about jobs and bringing news from home. Some jobs, like being a personal assistant or driver, often require a recommendation from someone, so this is good if someone comes to the restaurant and wants to help you. The African braiding shops in big cities can work in the same way for African women.

THE SOMETIMES PAINFUL JOURNEY TO CITIZENSHIP

While I have now completed my journey to citizenship, some in my family are still on that journey and the way is not always easy. It saddens me to see many Africans in the US without legal papers and no program to help them. Some came here to stay alive and to try to bring hope to their families. They miss their parents, children, and even spouses. It is very sad to see people in this position.

My older sister Gnale and I had the honor of bringing all our family members to America, but only a couple of us are US citizens today. My sister came to America in March 1994, six months pregnant with my nephew Baba. She gave birth to him in Bronx, New York, in June 1994 and after 14 years, she is still here with her husband and three more children back in Africa.

Though I sponsored her immigration status right before Bill Clinton left the White House, it is supposed to take anywhere from 12 to 15 years of waiting to get citizenship according to immigration law. Now with no other solution, can you believe that soon it will be my sister's own son who will be saving his mother? When he turns 18 in four years, he will be able to give a resident card to his mother in six months to a year so she can go home for the first time in 18 or 19 years even though she has been sending money and everything else all this time. There are many, many Africans in this same situation.

"ARE YOU STILL AFRICAN?"

Sometimes when I go home, I am stopped by someone's mother who hasn't heard from her son in a long time. "Is he still African?" she will ask in a quiet voice. It seems like a silly question, but I understand what she means.

Sometimes I simply hug the woman rather than deliver the news I know would hurt her—her son has forgotten about his African family at home and his heritage. Even worse is when a man has left a wife and children behind to find a better life for the family and he becomes silent and never returns home.

I have been here long enough to feel comfortable taking part in American culture but not so much that I forget who I am or where I come from. To think that you can live here and try to live in Africa at the same time though will not work. You must embrace the culture you now live in. Our African-American ladies are good at reminding us that we cannot expect people to act the same way that they do at home. As some would say, "This ain't Africa!" And they are right. We are in a new place and while we must hold on to our African spirit, we must also understand American ways as well.

As I said, at first, the African evaluates every move in America based on money and usually African money at that. After a while, he begins to forget about the African money and starts thinking in dollars. Life will take a turn on itself and bring him to this place. Though his heart may be in Africa with his parents and friends, his mind and hands are in America and if he is going to succeed, he must concentrate on what is going on here. He doesn't want to falter and have to go home and struggle having thrown away what might be his only chance for a better life.

Due to that focus, some black Americans might look at an African and think he doesn't have anything because he isn't displaying some of the material things that signal prosperity in African-American culture. You might see an African here walking down the street and think he looks like nothing, but he might have $30,000-$40,000 saved so that he can help people back at home.

To that man, helping his people is more important than designer clothes or a new car. None of that means anything to him. The outside look is not the goal. This man has the big picture of all the people behind him, praying and hoping that he will succeed so that they can have a chance. He is putting on his old jeans thinking of how he can save the people back at home. If he just has something to put on and keep going, then he is fine. He will wear shoes from Payless rather than overspend. When he gets the BIG money, like hundreds of thousands of dollars, then you might see him looking a little better.

These are the kinds of Africans, myself included, who once worried about "staying African." Some of these types will shy away from getting too involved with black Americans because they think this is going to throw them into a way of thinking that is too expensive and will make them forget the goals they came to this country with.

I have seen many men whose focus gradually became only to take care of themselves. People will begin to say, "Has he called his parents lately? Has he forgotten them? Is he focused on himself?" I hope that I will never become that way. The African gets blessing from taking care of his parents and elders, doing things for them even if they didn't ask.

This is something I have had to discuss when entering into friendships and relationships with black Americans. Africans believe in splitting everything with family members. The African-American mindset doesn't always think this way. In some families, it is every man or woman for himself or herself. Each person is buying clothes and cars and if the African isn't careful, he'll be thinking about doing it, too. Before long, it will be difficult to think about sending something to your parents when you see so many more things that you could have for yourself.

And when it comes to relationships, well, that gets really interesting. It takes a lot of love and understanding for an

African American to understand his or her African spouse's desire to share with family as well as modestly do things for themselves here in the US.

For this reason, Africans usually seek out other Africans and stay within their own groups, especially at first. In the beginning, most Africans try to marry African women to help keep them on their traditional path of caring for people back home. However, there can be one problem once the African marries an African woman here: now his wife is trying to help her parents back at home, too! Most Africans are both helping out people at home and have the ambition to be able to do something big in Africa. And on top of that, there is the care of daily needs that must be met.

This kind of situation is a problem because the lady is worrying about her family, but she's not concerned about any bills here in America. She might take her money only for herself and her parents back home. She is the parents' stock and now they are benefiting from it. The husband? Well, he had just better pay the rest of it the best he can. Though most African men won't mind sending something to his in-laws now and then, every week or every month can be a bit much. From this perspective, we can understand how the African-American wife might feel when her husband is trying to send money home.

However, if this woman starts complaining all the time about sending this and that for her parents it can become a big argument. This is especially true if the wife's family is all bringing their problems to her in hopes that she can get the husband to fix them. We Mandingo believe that once you are married, you are married to your husband and are then part of his family. Love and compromise will then help you build a family together.

A GOOD WOMAN CAN BE HARD TO FIND

Though a man can come to America with a heart to succeed, nothing can complicate things more than entering a marriage with the wrong woman. If you're the only one of your family in America, there won't be anyone to help sort things out for you. If you are marrying an African-American woman, there might not be any father to express your interest to and if there is, the woman's father may not want to talk to "that African." Still many African men feel that marrying an African-American woman is better, even though the cultural differences sometimes lead to misunderstandings.

Though the African-American woman may not have a family to pay for like the African woman, she may be used to spending too much money. She might not understand about the African husband helping people back home. Many African-American women will work hard and help to accomplish the husband's dream project back in Africa even if she doesn't understand why he feels so passionate about it. Though people talk about people marrying for green cards, I would hope that no one is trying to do that. It takes a lot more than that to make a relationship work. There has to be some understanding.

THE AFRICAN'S BIGGEST FEAR

While leaving Africa and coming to America can be a scary thing, there is one thing even more frightening: going home as a failure. It's so terrible a thought that many Africans stop communicating with the families and never go home again if they do not do well here. When people back at home see this and they know that you are not communicating with your family, they will lose respect for you. It is almost like you are dead.

Even the Africans here in the US won't talk too much to you. They are afraid that this way of thinking will rub off on them. Some think they are expected to bring thousands and thousands of dollars if they come home after being in America so long, but in truth people don't care about the money, they just want to see the person and know that they are all right.

LIFE IN THE COMPOUND

The reason the African in America doesn't want to fail is he has seen his own father, brothers, and uncles struggle all their lives. They get up each morning and try to find some work to do to keep from asking someone to give them money to feed their children. This getting up and finding something to do, even when there is nothing to do, is part of staying alive, part of showing that you're trying.

When my father was a minivan driver, my family ate very well. People would send their kids "to play" at our house around meal time so that they could have something to eat. In the compound, everyone can see who has a fire and food cooking in the common kitchen and who doesn't. If there is a place with no fire and food, my mother and the other ladies who have something to share will tell all the children without to wash their hands and come and eat. The women are very observant and know how to put something extra together and send it over with the children so the rest of the family can eat something.

Many people will live in the same compound for most of their lives or at least as long as they can afford the rent. When I was growing up, rent was $7 a month. It is $15 or more today. There are people who have made it big, but they still live in the compound. There was a man who used to sew. The man is big time today. His clothes sell in France and on the Internet. He has his own Mercedes, a driver and owns four or five compounds of his own. His children go to private school, and his wife is well taken care of. He still has 50 or more technicians making clothes for him. All this, and he still lives in a compound himself.

MAKING IT OUT OF THE VILLAGE

People in Africa are always trying to find some business, some way to be an entrepreneur. There are plentiful natural resources throughout Africa, but it is difficult for the everyday African to be able to profit from it. Diamonds are not that big anymore although people have made their money in that over time. Gold is still there, but again it is difficult to access and sell. This is in the hands of the government now. Agriculture of course is big, but do you know what one of the biggest businesses you will now see in Africa is? Selling goods from Asia!

That's right. Africa is the second largest continent in area and population behind Asia, and China knows it. Wholesalers buy from Asians and sell on the street every day. Sometimes African women will go together and take a trip to China, Korea, or Taiwan to get merchandise. Together, they may be able to buy enough that the price of item drops from $3 to $1. Now these women will get rich.

Agriculture is still going strong although not long ago, cocoa plantations were accused of modern day slavery for overworking their workers. Ivory Coast now has its own city bus. It is the first of many. These are the things that the African thinks about when he wants to spend money that could help change his country and even the world. As we come together, I think African Americans can do just that.

CHAPTER EIGHT

African in America: One Man's Journey

Not one moment of my life has been boring or without meaning. I credit that to my African upbringing and to my parents who instilled in me that I was valuable to the world.

I was born and raised in Abidjan, Ivory Coast in West Africa. My parents came to Ivory Coast from Guinea and both were of the Mandingo bloodline. As a young man, I learned to speak many languages including French and attended school in Abidjan. The only language I didn't learn was English, which would later prove to be a stumbling block, though I did overcome it.

There had been enough training, support, and love for me to become my own keeper. I knew that I could accomplish whatever I desired and that it was God's will for me to accomplish my goals.

I come from a large family of five sisters and three brothers. Of all my siblings, five of us are living in the US today. I have two sons: the youngest lives in Chicago and my eldest son attend college in Virginia. I am very proud; however, the road to where I am today hasn't been an easy one.

In the August of 1987, I arrived at John F. Kennedy Airport. My bag held my few belongings: three pairs of pants, a few shirts and a jacket. The city buzzed with activity as I stepped out into the hustle and bustle of New York City. Everyone seemed to be going somewhere or rushing to meet someone. Everyone, except me.

After the ordeal of passing through Customs and being cleared by immigration, I now faced New York City. A yellow cab appeared. I got in, but when the driver demanded to know where I wanted to go, I could not understand his language. Though I knew some English, it was the proper English of books and the man's New Yorker dialect confused me. I was 25 years old, but I felt like a child again for a moment: alone in a strange country with no place to go and no way to communicate.

Once we'd tried and failed several times to understand each other, the man in the taxi suddenly shouted, "Africa!" as though he had hit the jackpot. He seemed to know where to take me then; an area of Manhattan where he knew many Africans lived. He dropped me off on 165th and Broadway with a look that said he'd done all he could and I'd have to go on from here … alone.

I stepped out of the cab into the chaos of people mingling through Harlem. I stared into the eyes of strangers, repeating the word that had meant so much to the cab driver. "Africa! Africa!" I said over and over. Finally, someone understood my despair and pointed to the apartment building in front of me.

"Up! Up!" they said.

Still scared and tired from my journey, I did as I was told and went into the building and up the stairs. There I found a world that was wonderful and beautiful; there I found people who could understand my language.

The first gentleman I met was from Mali, the same area of West Africa that I am from. I was thrilled and explained that I had just arrived alone and knew no one. I asked if he could help me settle in. He took me upstairs where seven men sat talking. He introduced me around and asked if anyone needed a second driver on the night-shift taxi run.

This sounds amazing when I tell the story to some Americans, but this is African solidarity. No matter where you meet another African, he can never be a stranger. I had nothing to fear because they had traveled the same road I was on and had one day arrived at an American airport with very little. Everyone was willing to help me, the newcomer to America; the newcomer to Harlem.

This is the natural instinct, attitude and respect of the African spirit. We believe in helping one another. I was the seventh man in this one room apartment; they ran the room like a small business. Everyone shared the housing expense, paying ten dollars each per week to stay there.

In the room was a leader, the head of operations, with three seniors beneath him who helped the business run smoothly. It wasn't about profit, but about helping the newcomers, knowing that they would be blessed and appreciated one day when we all made it big in the world.

We were running a cab business. As back at home in Africa, we were entrepreneurs making a living for ourselves by driving people around. Our operation had three four-door sedans. We took turns driving and sleeping, with the back-up person driving whenever someone needed to sleep.

Watching the others, I knew that if they could do this, then I could do it, too. And I did. Three days after arriving in

Harlem and after some training, I was driving one of the cabs. Though I had driven at home and my own father had owned a car business, I felt a little nervous at first. I wanted to do everything right, just as my African brothers had instructed me. My English was very limited and my understanding of directions for driving was different than the American way. The main thing I had to understand was what it meant when someone asked, "How much do I pay you?"

I can't tell you how many times I got lost at night in the cab and the passengers had to direct me or some stranger on the street gave me directions. It took a good month or more before I was at ease at driving the cab. I slowly learned my way around, driving the "Gypsy Cab" through Harlem, the Bronx, Brooklyn, and Queens.

I was everywhere. Unfortunately that meant I saw some of everything. I was held up twice: the robber held a gun to my head for the money I'd made the first time and the second time I was two blocks away from the Apollo Theater when I was robbed. Both times, I know that it was only the grace of God that saved my life.

Driving a cab wasn't fun, but it was a start in America and helped me to pay bills and learn English. After the robberies, I stopped driving the cab and began to focus on finding a safer position so that I could go to school, learn more English, and make my way to a university, my new goal. There was some other opportunity for advancement in this country; I just had to find it.

By this time, I was almost 27 years old. I found a car wash job on the west side of Manhattan. I had to work two weeks without being paid and never received my first paycheck. Talk about a trial period! It was one of the worst struggles I have ever encountered up to today. When I think about what I endured during the time, tears come to my eyes.

For many days, I slept but did not eat. I said nothing to my African roommates. When I finally received a paycheck, it was for $300, the most money I had ever seen in my life. It was a sweat shop job, very physical and not as much money as when I drove the cab, but when it was all on the check at once, it really seemed like a lot. I had to pay my room, board, transportation and food with that pay which after the first check was $150 for six days a week from 8 AM to 5 PM.

Sometimes I ran out of money and found myself walking the more than 120 city blocks to my job in Manhattan. I'd leave my tiny Harlem apartment early in the morning to arrive at work at 8 AM. By the time I got there, my legs felt like they'd been set on fire. Walking to work on days when I ran out of money proved to be a very painful workout.

Other times, I couldn't afford to buy a sandwich, not to mention a full course meal. When the hunger pains hit, I just got food the best way I could, even sometimes scavenging for food behind Spanish restaurants on Broadway. I'd eat whatever half-eaten meal was on top of the dumpster rather than go and beg my roommates who had already done so much for me. Besides, I was a man and wanted to be responsible for myself. I knew my brothers would help me if I asked them, but I also knew that each of them had gone through what I was dealing with then.

I was determined to be successful and saw my plight as temporary. Every night in Harlem when I was walking, I began to meet other Africans and socialize and make new friends.

The car wash manager began to send me home early with any hours not worked deducted from my $150 a week pay. My roommates would try to get me to drive the cab again, but that was unsafe and wouldn't allow for me to learn English and attend college. I had to stay focused on my dream.

Time went by with me working varied hours at the car wash; the opportunity I had been waiting for came along—English classes in Harlem! Classes were from 6-9 PM, perfect for my schedule. I attended three nights a week and within a few months I was making progress.

Through this class, I quickly realized that education was the key to advancement in America. In Africa, there are many people with degrees, but there aren't always jobs for them to be placed into. In the US, the jobs are there, but not many people are seeking the education.

For several years I attended the English course until I could excel in speaking and writing English. Then I started sending out job applications to be a security guard so that I could work and study at the same time.

Three years after arriving in New York, I was hired as a security guard in Manhattan. This was a dream come true. With my new job, I could now move to my own place in the Bronx and prepare for my brothers Kaba and Moussa to arrive from Africa. I didn't want them to experience what I'd gone through when I arrived. My youngest sister would join us a year later.

This was a family thing. My eldest sister, Gnale, now deceased, helped my siblings to get to the US and take advantage of the opportunities here. In the meantime, I worked as a security guard all over New York, from the Empire State Building to both towers of the former World Trade Center. I worked these places for eight months at a time, including ten-hour shifts on the George Washington Bridge alone. This was frightening at times, but I did what I had to do.

A year later, I was ready to work toward my new dream of becoming an aircraft mechanic. Now that I had my siblings to support, it was time to dream bigger. As the eldest in our home, I did my best in helping my siblings get situated. Kaba attended high school while Moussa drove a gypsy cab, despite my warnings to him about the dangers. Namassa cooked for us until I could find something that would bring her an income. When I wasn't working my night shift security job, I was researching colleges with morning classes.

The College of Aeronautics at LaGuardia Airport offered an accredited Aviation Technician degree and practice toward becoming a federal licensed aircraft mechanic. Another program offered a certificate in Utica, New York, that took less time than the LaGuardia program. Before I could enter either program though, I learned that I would need a high school diploma.

This was another setback, but not an impossible situation. I took my GED in French with an English portion on the test. I applied for school, but did not pass the entrance exam. I took it again and failed, but due to my perseverance and God's mercy, I passed the third time.

In 1994, almost seven years since my arrival, I started at the College of Aeronautics at LaGuardia Airport in Queens. Now that my siblings were here, I was determined to make it through at any cost. It was my responsibility.

It wasn't easy. I had to learn technical English, which was nothing like the everyday English I'd finally grown to understand. My schedule—working all night as a security guard and then rushing to classes—posed a challenge as well. Many times, I had to leave straight from the job site and go directly to class. I slept four hours a day in those times and studied some on my night job.

The learning didn't come easy either. Some days I simply couldn't understand what my instructors were saying, even after they'd explained a concept more than once. I found a good group of friends to study with and this proved beneficial. I wasn't socializing much with my African friends, but they understood and supported me in my goals. I spent most of my free time either studying or being with my family.

Though things were difficult, I excelled, ending my first semester with a 3.5 GPA and on the Faculty Honor List. My older sister Namassa had been six months pregnant when she arrived and my niece Poupette had moved in also from Africa. My nephew Moussa Sanogo was born while we lived in that house in the Bronx. My own son, William Mory Sano, visited us often during this time as well. His mother, an African-American woman with a great deal of knowledge about African culture and tradition, gave me an intelligent wonderful son who I am proud of until this day.

Though my responsibilities were growing, I completed all my courses and passed the Federal Aviation Administration exams. It was a wonderful achievement, but it was clouded by the great loss of my eldest sister Gnale who passed away unexpectedly after a few days of illness.

It was a sad time for the whole family, but very difficult for me. Exams were the last thing on my mind, yet I had two days of oral, written, and practical task testing ahead of me. The loss of my sister broke my morale; however, I was able to score 84 out of 100 points. This gave me my Associate degree and my Federal Aviation Aircraft Mechanic license in 1997.

United Airlines contacted me immediately through the career center at the college due to the school's recommendation. I accepted the offer and started an internship which took me to San Francisco, Denver, Chicago, Oakland, and Indianapolis. All my expenses were paid and at the end of twelve weeks, I received a certificate of completion.

After that, I accepted a position with United Airlines in Indianapolis, Indiana. This meant leaving my family behind in New York. My sister (the younger Namassa—I have two sisters with the same name) got married and moved to Philadelphia and my niece got married and moved to Atlanta. The older Namassa soon followed me with my nephew to Indianapolis, where we lived comfortably in a 5000 square foot, four bedroom homes with a two car garage. I'd come a long way from sharing one bedroom with six other men!

I worked at United Airlines in Indianapolis until 2003. The terrorist attack against America on September 11, 2001, brought airplane travel to a halt. All airlines started to lay off employees since people were afraid to fly. The US government urged all aviation employees to go back to school for more training, preferably in a different field. They would pay all expenses for up to two years of training. Once again, I began to research programs to attend.

I returned to college in Indiana and earned an Associate of Applied Science in Biomedical Electronics two years later. This meant I could work in any hospital as a biomedical technician.

With two degrees behind me, I was now ready to live up to my full potential.

Upon graduation, I moved back to New York with my brothers, who now lived in Harlem. The older Namassa who had been with me in Indianapolis moved to Chicago to work in an African braiding shop owned by a longtime friend.

About this time, the idea for this book formed in my head as I began to consider the divide between Africans and African Americans. There was a difference. I had experienced it in each of the different places I had lived. This was something that I wanted to help change. It was then that I began to write, especially during the period when I was unemployed and looking for work.

Ironically, the job I got called for was as an aviation mechanic at LaGuardia airport. That was in 2005. Today, I am contracted out as an aircraft mechanic by any company in the US or around the globe.

Though my journey to success took almost twenty years, it shows that anyone can make it if they never give up on their dreams. This book is just another way of me stepping out on a dream and taking a chance. That's just who I am and part of my African roots, which emphasize steadfastness and patience.

In February 2008, I made a trip that I had been dreaming of—a trip back to Abidjan for a visit. My family and I had worked hard. It was time to be refreshed with Africa. It was just what I needed to keep me on track. It recharged my dream of bringing Africans and African-Americans together and overcoming our differences.

Africa taught me to be strong and love myself. God taught me to have faith and love others. I hope that you will accomplish all of your dreams, too. And don't forget to represent Africa!

My struggles didn't hinder me from reaching my goals. I pursued my dreams and God made it possible for me to realize them. Keep trying until you are successful. Grow into your full potential. Connect with your fellow African family. Let's show the world that Africans have and will continue to make a difference in the world.

And remember, just when you think things are hopeless, there's always another chance.

CHAPTER NINE

MEETING ON THE MIDDLE OF THE BRIDGE

Though it is my hope that American blacks and African immigrants can bridge the divide between them, the truth is that all Africans are not Americans, nor do they wish to be. All black Americans do not consider themselves "African," desiring instead to know specifically the place and people where they come from. So where does that leave us?

Unfortunately, in some communities, fear and misunderstanding have turned black and African relations into a boxing match. Even the children are fighting.[31] Some immigrants think that the term "African-American" is an ill-fitting garment, unsuited to their specific needs of language barriers and cultural and moral differences. American blacks see Africans being hired for good jobs and admitted to even Ivy League colleges[32] in the name of "diversity" and feel the term African-American might not be narrow enough.

---

[31] Johnson, Rob. "African Immigrants, Black Americans at Odds." *The Roanoke Times.* 5 Aug. 2009
<http://www.roanoke.com/news/roanoke/wb/159336>.
[32] Hayes, Edward. "African immigrants, affirmative action, and Harvard University." *Examiner.com.* 5 Aug. 2009 <http://www.examiner.com/x-3865-Chicago-Public-Education-Examiner~y2009m6d20-African-immigrants-affirmative-action-and-Harvard-University>.

With all the emerging pundits and politicians ready to choose sides, do we still have a chance to meet on the middle of the bridge, let alone cross the gap between blacks and Africans in America?

Absolutely. In the end, it won't be what people call us that make the difference, but how we react as America once again redefines race and begins to embrace culture instead.

"It is not simply a matter of white Americans and black Americans confronting a shared past. It is a redefinition of who is white, who is black, who is African-American, and how we should treat each other," says Ghanaian Kobina Aidoo, 32, who has taken his film, *The Neo-African-Americans*, to college campuses throughout the country, including Princeton.[33]

Aidoo feels certain that Barack Obama is the bridge to redefining race. While I agree that the elect of President Obama has sparked a new discussion in America on race and blackness, the journey over the bridge must be made by each individual alone. With that said, there are several factors that may help speed up the journey: marriage, marketing, and migration will help us across the hyphenated landscape of American race relations.

MARRIAGE

Emeka Aniukwu, a 35-year-old Nigerian met his current wife, Sonya Roberts, 25, in a grocery store in 2005. Though both had been misinformed about each other's culture, their feelings

---

[33] Braun, Bob. "Washington's African Immigrants See Obama Redefining Race." *NJ.com*. 5 Aug. 2009
<http://blog.nj.com/njv_bob_braun/2009/01/washingtons_african_immigrants.html>.

helped them overcome it. Emeka taught Sonya about Nigeria and she taught him about African-American culture.

"Talk to people, stop showing ugly face and don't be shy about your accent," he advised African immigrants. "Most of the media coverage about Africa is all about hunger, diseases, and war, so what do you expect? People are curious and just want to know, so calm down and educate them as much as you can,"[34] says Aniukwu, whose wedding was attended by Nigerians, African Americans, whites, and Hispanics. He and his bride honeymooned in China. This is the face of the new "black" couple: global, cross-cultural and able to communicate.

Will love be a major force in bring Ivorians, Ghanaians, Nigerians, Ethiopians, South Africans, and natives of the over 53 African countries to bridge the growing gap between them and African Americans? Eric Foner, a Columbia University historian seems to think so, agreeing that race defined as we know it may be on borrowed time.

"I guess one of the questions will have to be what happens in the next generation or two," said Foner. "In America, marriage is the great solvent. Are they [African immigrants] going to melt into the African-American population? Most likely yes."[35]

---

[34] McLaughlin, Eliott C. "Continental divide separates Africans, African-Americans." *CNN.com.* 5 Aug. 2009
<http://www.cnn.com/2009/US/07/14/africans.in.america/index.html>.
[35] Roberts, *New York Times.*

MARKETS

According to the U.S. African Consumer Segment[36] study, African immigrants wield $50 billion in purchasing power. Even more amazing is the fact that this market is virtually untapped. Just as commercials began to bounce to hip-hop beats as retailers scrambled for black dollars in recent decades, we can expect to see marketing with the buying preferences of African immigrants in mind.

As Wal-Mart unveils its Spanish-language banners to appeal to Hispanic buyers[37], one can only imagine what the future might hold. Will going to the grocery store eventually be like walking through the airport with each shopper greeted in their preferred language with a pre-selected marketing campaign?

It could happen, but probably not for a while. In the meantime, we'll all be sharing media and marketing together, with companies waiting for us to speak so they can see which pitch we get. In the end, we might actually learn something about each other through the media. With billions in shared consumer dollars at stake, corporations will find a way to market both racially and culturally, knowing that without a soundtrack, a black face and a good price will appeal to both African-born and American-born blacks.

---

[36] Morse, David. "The US African Consumer Segment." *African Immigrant Presentation.* US African Chamber of Commerce. 5 Aug. 2009 <http://www.99clients.com/USACC/African_Immigrant_Presentation(2).pdf>.

[37] "African Immigrants Represent Untapped Consumer Resource." *Retailer Daily.* 5 Aug. 2009 <http://www.retailerdaily.com/entry/13855/african-immigrants-untapped-resource/>.

The outsourcing of technology to Asia and the immigration of many of Africa's great minds are coloring the consumer landscape in new shades. Retailers are embracing the reality of a diverse black buyer. It's up to us to pay it forward with a little patience and love for each other, knowing that despite the well-crafted sales pitches, in the end, when people look at us, they see a black person, no matter where we were born.

MIGRATION

While the migration of over a million Africans to the US has made some blacks uncomfortable, they may find themselves puzzled over a new population trend: reverse migration.

You read it right. Many recent US African immigrants are going back home where they can live a decent life with less stress.

"The people I know here work two or three jobs just to make ends meet, while in Kenya—despite its problems—people seem happier," explained the head of one African association.[38]

African immigrants, who often arrive in America with advanced degrees that aren't recognized, often have to repeat their education to get the jobs they want. Perhaps in tough economic times, it is easier to go home and use their skills.

"Right now I'm feeling no stress, no anxiety," said James Odhiambo, 34, relaxing in his family home in a western

---

[38] McCrummen, Stephanie. "A Better Life Beckons in Africa U.S. Downturn Drives Immigrant Professionals Back Home." *The Washington Post*. 5 Aug. 2009 <http://www.washingtonpost.com/wp-dyn/content/article/2009/05/25/AR2009052502313.html?hpid=topnews>.

Kenyan city along the shores of Lake Victoria. "Think of it this way: When I was in the U.S., I was close to 300 pounds. Now, I'm like 200. The biggest thing for me was quality of life."[39]

Odhiambo's wife has dropped four dress sizes, too. Their two young daughters are gathering the courage to go outside and play without being afraid. As India and China have found a way to prosper at home, perhaps some of the recent African immigrants will find new success at home as well. With the numbers of immigrants reduced, Africans and American blacks will need each other more than ever. As the new black melting pot sizzles and simmers, one thing is certain: the world is changing.

Both the African I left behind and the America some were born into are no longer the same. What it means to be black in America or African American will likely change, too. Let's all seek to compromise and try to understand the fears, hurts, and history we have in common as well as cherishing our differences.

While a person with a strong national identity may not want to be referred to under the blanket term of African-American, understand the journey for blacks in America to express their African heritage at all. We have to come together, talk honestly, and see both sides. Black Americans have a rich tradition of civil rights and making strides through programs and legislation. Many African countries lack the infrastructure to assist their citizens on that level, so African immigrants may seem to skip the rallies and go to a study session instead.

---

[39] McCrummen, Stephanie. *The Washington Post*.

Education is the economic equalizer for many Africans, yet we too have something to learn from our cousins about mobilizing political power.

Through cooperation, communication and kinship, we can decide how race and culture will be defined instead of waiting for someone else to do it for us. So seek out the African-Americans in your community and ask them to join you for the first of many days of discovery.

I think the day is coming when I will simply be Keleti Sanon and as Martin Luther King, Jr. dreamed, my character will be judged before my color. Until then though, join me on the bridge and remember that whatever happened in Africa in the past still affects us in America today. May we find a brighter future, Africans and African Americans together!

RECOMMENDED RESOURCES

Books

Franklin, John Hope. *From Slavery to Freedom: A History of African Americans.* 8th Ed. New York: Knopf, 2000.

Ghazvinian, John. *Untapped: The Scramble for African Oil.* New York: Harcourt, 2007.

Haskins, James, Kathleen Benson, and Floyd Cooper. *Bound for America: the Forced Migration of Africans to the New World.* 1st Ed. New York: Harper Collins, 1999.

Heard, J. Norman. *The Black Frontiersman: Adventures of Negroes of American Native Americans (1528-1918).* New York: The John Day Company, 1969.

Jones, Maxine Delores, and McCarthy, Kevin M., *African Americans in Florida.* Sarasota, FL: Pineapple Press, Inc., 1993.

Rediker, Marcus. *The Slave Ship: A Human History.* 1st Ed. New York: Viking Adult, 2007.

Terrell, John Upton, *Estevanico the Black.* Los Angeles: Westernlore Press, 1968.

ONLINE RESOURCES

"Yearbook of Immigration Statistics 2007." *Department of Homeland Security.*
<http://www.dhs.gov/ximgtn/statistics/publications/LPR07.shtm>.

Roberts, Sam. "More Africans Enter U.S. Than in Days of Slavery." *The New York Times.*
<http://www.nytimes.com/2005/02/21/nyregion/21africa.html?_r=1&scp=1&sq=more%20africans%20voluntarily%20than%20slavery&st=cse>.

About the Author

Keleti Sanon arrived from Africa with no common language, no family, and nowhere to go. Twenty years later, he is a college graduate two times over, a professional aircraft mechanic, and a man with a passion for bringing Africans and African Americans closer together.

In his years driving a cab on the streets of New York City and traveling the country with United Airlines, Sanon realized that much more than a hyphen separated Africans from their black cousins. Myths, media, and misunderstanding on both sides kept those of African descent in America from celebrating their culture.

After being asked by a non-Black person how he felt about American blacks being called African American when they "know nothing about Africa," Sanon determined to share the gift of Africa with his cousins so that no one would ever have to ask him such a thing again.

Sanon has participated in African associations across the country and continues to visit his native Ivory Coast to help bring hope and economic change. His is the voice of all of Africa, crying out to those who sprung from her shores. "Come home in your heart," Sanon says. "We must give Africa—and ourselves—another chance."

Please send comments to Keleti at:
Kingsamory@hotmail.com and visit him on the web at:
www.Keletisanon.com or www.windowofafrica.com.

www.ingramcontent.com/pod-product-compliance
Lightning Source LLC
Chambersburg PA
CBHW051805040426
42446CB00007B/529